ART AND SURVIVAL
Patricia Johanson's Environmental Projects

by Caffyn Kelley

with an introduction by Lucy R. Lippard

Islands Institute

ISLANDS INSTITUTE OF INTERDISCIPLINARY STUDIES

Salt Spring Island, BC, Canada

www.islandsinstitute.com

Library and Archives Canada Cataloguing in Publication

Kelley, Caffyn, 1957-
       Art and survival : Patricia Johanson's environmental
projects / by Caffyn Kelley ; with an introduction by Lucy
Lippard.

Includes bibliographical references and index.
ISBN 0-9738332-0-3

  1   Johanson, Patricia, 1940- 2. Nature in art. I. Johanson,

Patricia, 1940-   II. Title.
N6537.J57K44 2005   709'.2   C2005-904175-7

Cover photo by William Pankey

Book and cover design by Jonathon Nix

Image assembly by Gerrit Goossen

Copy editing by Karen Bjornland

Printed in Hong Kong.

Frontispiece: *Ellis Creek Water Recycling Facility: Pond D: Mouse*, 8⅝" x 9⅛", ink and pencil, 2004

CONTENTS

PANORAMA

Introduction by Lucy R. Lippard

LOOKING AND READING THROUGH THIS LONG-AWAITED BOOK, I'M ASTOUNDED ALL over again, as I have been over the years when called upon to focus on Patricia Johanson's art and ideas. Her achievements on the ground and in the imagination are breathtaking. Of all the artists (so many of them women) who have become known over the last few decades for large-scale public art in/with nature – what is now called "eco-art," Johanson stands out as a seldom-acknowledged pioneer. Her writings of the late 1960s, when she was still in her twenties, are a cornucopia of possibilities for environmental art and planning that are still being "discovered" today.

Johanson's public art offers a rare sense of being present at the vortex of culture and nature. Her images, drawn from precise botanical and biological sources, loop, uncoil, and crawl elegantly across the land, evoking evolution, life, and movement. The forms are in fact so vital, so life-filled, that they provoke more of the same from those who use them. I think of the pictures of children leaping from one section to another of *Fair Park Lagoon* in Dallas, beside contented birds, ducks, turtles – all in their own ways following the rhythms Johanson has outlined for them; or the bewitched viewers drinking in unprecedented views across the top of the rainforest canopy in Brazil,

Facing page: Longshore Barrier Spit at *Endangered Garden*, San Francisco

accompanied by playful monkeys and tropical birds; or the endangered species slowly returning to Candlestick Cove in California, nestling into life-supporting habitats in the images of the San Francisco Garter Snake and the tiny Ribbon Worm.

Like the music that once absorbed her talents, her work has a distinct temporal element, not just because it is large enough to extend and expand lived experience, but because it incorporates time and history on multiple overlapping scales, from the geological continuum that formed the bedrock to the brief lives and transformations of butterflies. The shifting patterns and kinesthetic macro-imagery unfold into a series of experiences rather than a single picture. She talks about the very multiplicity of every place, which allows everyone (all living things) an entrance into it, when the way is shown. And she has shown the way in Brazil, South Korea, and Kenya, as well as in the United States.

Although photographers have delved into the landscape of "humanature," public artists are often content to provide a static oasis of nature within a cultural context. Some parks and many gardens actually seem to resist the flux of nature and social change. Johanson, on the other hand, is so familiar with both processes that she can absorb them unselfconsciously into her work. "We tend to enshrine and protect our resources," she has written. "Ultimately, daily life is more important than a Sunday outing. It goes to the issue of how we really live. Do you have one good experience, and then go back to a tedious existence, or is your daily life enriched and enhanced? What I've been trying to do is dissolve the hierarchies, and get everything on the same level – the art, the people, the plants, the soil, the water."

Heir to the vague but open training that characterizes fine arts education, Johanson has always thought past the boundaries of her wide-ranging disciplines – art, biology, landscape architecture, agronomy, highway and city planning – slowly acquiring the expertise that has led to her respected standing in several fields. Most importantly, the interconnections she establishes between the ground and the image are visual reflections of ecological principles. She has lived rurally most of her adult life, isolated from the art world in which she once fully participated. This distance has proved beneficial. Looking around a familiar place year after year, living over and over

Facing page: *Park for the Amazon Rainforest*, Obidos, Brazil, model of canopy walkway, 1992

again through changing seasons there, offers an informed overview and passion for detail unavailable from outside sources. Living in Buskirk, New York, has endowed Johanson with a sense of the local that can be translated to the unfamiliar places where she is commissioned to make public art. More important, it enables her to conceive this functional art with social consequences, and to communicate this sense of the local, of where we stand, to the people who will live with her work, wherever it is. In the process of working with a sewer plant, a baywalk, a highway, she opens up to public use and comprehension chunks of a city's infrastructure – those places usually quarantined behind chain link fences. In addition, she offers ingenious engineering solutions as a result of seeing "the city as an ecological art form," and "the world as art."

The plant and reptile/amphibian worlds have provided Johanson's vocabulary – snakes in particular, with their edge of perceived danger, their beneficial role in ecosystems, their resemblance to roads and water in motion, their wide-ranging symbolic significances in so many cultures. Their metaphorical journeys inform her basically linear practice as she draws in space on the land, creating trails in several senses. Walking is important not only to our physical health but it keeps us moving mentally as well; its rhythms, like those of breathing, lead us through landscape and place, in and out of mindfulness, never failing to offer new sights and insights. One of my favorites among her recent works is *The Rocky Marciano Trail* in Brockton, Massachusetts. Here Johanson, known for her sensitivity to soil, animals, and plants, focuses on social issues, on a deteriorating New England factory town and its hero, the only man who might inspire residents to resist their economic fate. Finding the famous fighter's home abandoned, she bought it as the centerpiece of "Brockton Pride." Waterways and "green streets" follow Marciano's youthful running routes through his hometown, becoming the unifying threads of her project.

Johanson's working model *is* the ecosystem and survival is her core theme, one she knows all too well, personally and politically. Patience and flexibility are useful skills in life as well as in art. Exploring the survival strategies of plants and animals suggests ways in which her art can be of use as a healing force. But she never abandons beauty, well aware of its restorative properties. Nor does she compete with nature, content

Facing page: *Saggitaria platyphylla*, Fair Park Lagoon, Dallas, 235' x 175' x 12', gunite, plants and animals, 1981-1986

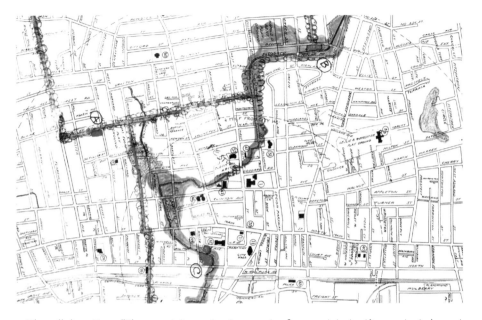

Left: Detail of Brockton Plan: Salisbury Brook (blue), magnet sites (orange), and green streets, 1998

Facing page: Vernal Pools *(Catagramma mionina): Park/ Amphibian Breeding Grounds/Edible Landscaping*, acrylic, gouache and ink on mylar, 42" x 44", 1992

with collaboration: "The most important aspect of my art is in the parts I do not design." In other words, like a conceptual artist, she calls attention to what is already there, framing its already vital existence, creating living landscapes. As Caffyn Kelley writes in the course of this excellent narrative, she "reconciles delicacy with strength, generosity with power, and creativity with consequence." There is no better and more crucially needed model for the future of our gardens, parks, and planet than Patricia Johanson's art.

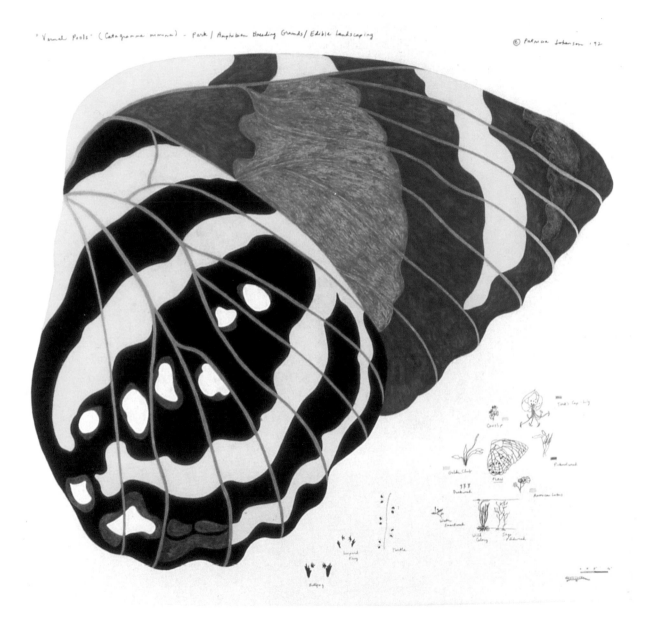

"Vernal Pools" (Catagramma minna) – Park / Amphibian Breeding Grounds / Edible Landscaping

© Patricia Johanson '92

xiii

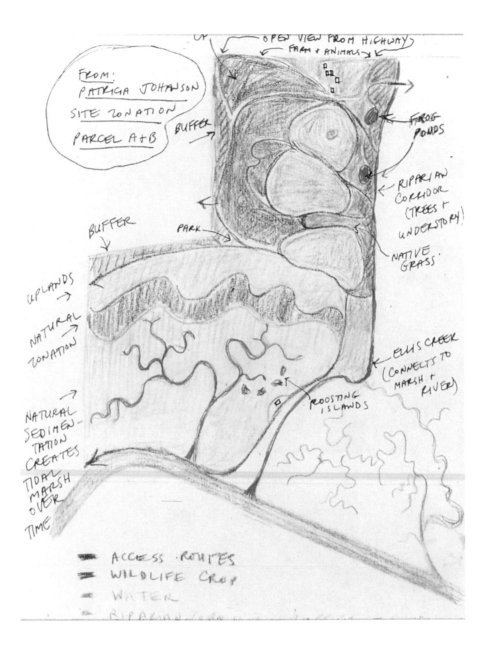

FROM:
PATRICIA JOHANSON
SITE ZONATION
PARCEL A+B

OPEN VIEW FROM HIGHWAY
FARM + ANIMALS

FROG PONDS

BUFFER

RIPARIAN CORRIDOR (TREES + UNDERSTORY)

BUFFER

PARK

NATIVE GRASS

UPLANDS

NATURAL ZONATION

ELLIS CREEK (CONNECTS TO MARSH + RIVER)

ROOSTING ISLANDS

NATURAL SEDIMENTATION CREATES TIDAL MARSH OVER TIME

ACCESS ROUTES
WILDLIFE CROP
WATER
RIPARIAN CORR.

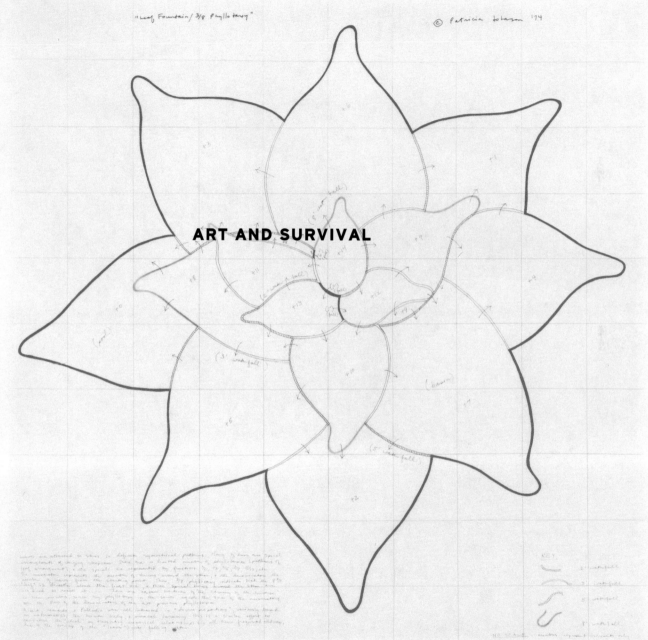

ART AND SURVIVAL

ART AND SURVIVAL

Previous pages, left: *Petaluma Wetlands Park and Water Recycling Facility: Site Zonation*, sketch for California Dogface Butterfly design, with polishing ponds (top) and Petaluma River and tidal wetlands park (bottom), 11" x 8½", ink and colored pencil, 2002

Right: *Leaf Fountain/3/8 Phyllotaxy*, 30" x 30", ink and charcoal, 1974. Collection: Museum of Modern Art, gift of R.L.B. Tobin

Facing page: *Saggitaria Platyphylla*, Fair Park Lagoon, Dallas, 235' x 175' x 12', gunite, plants, and animals, 1981-1986 (photo: William Pankey)

THE SURVIVAL OF OUR PLANET IS THREATENED. EACH DAY BRINGS NEWS OF ACCELERATING environmental crisis: global warming, species extinction, toxic wastes permeating earth and oceans. For over forty years, Patricia Johanson has patiently insisted that art can heal the earth. For more than twenty years, she has traveled around the world creating large-scale public projects that realize her radical, yet utterly practical vision. Johanson works with engineers, city planners, scientists and citizens' groups to build her art as functioning infrastructure for modern cities. In San Francisco, her sculpture is a sewer and a baywalk allowing public access to the waterfront, as well as life-supporting habitat for endangered species. Her art invites people into the Amazon rainforest and cleanses a polluted African river. In Korea, a 912-acre park creates territory for tigers, cranes, deer and bats, while linking the land with Korean cultural images. Every facet of a Johanson project is designed to perform multiple functions: cultural, social, infrastructural and environmental. Her designs satisfy deep human needs for beauty, belonging and historical memory, while they cleanse water, process sewage and create habitat.

Johanson became dissatisfied with making art for museums and galleries as she achieved a successful painting career in her twenties. While an undergraduate student

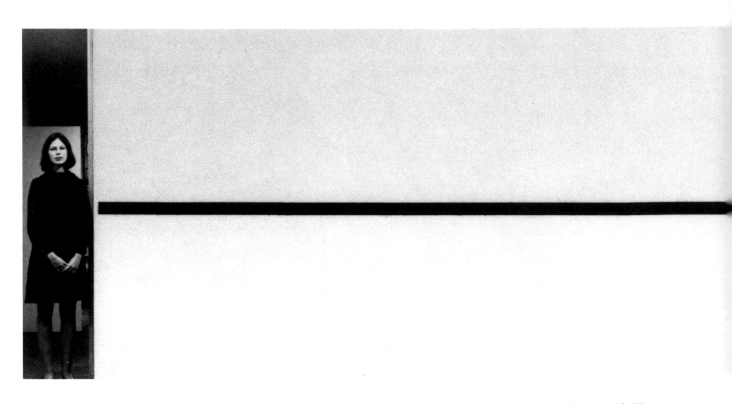

4

Above: Patricia Johanson with *Minor
Keith* at the Tibor de Nagy Gallery,
New York, 1967
8' 6" x 28', oil on canvas
(photo: William Sinclair)

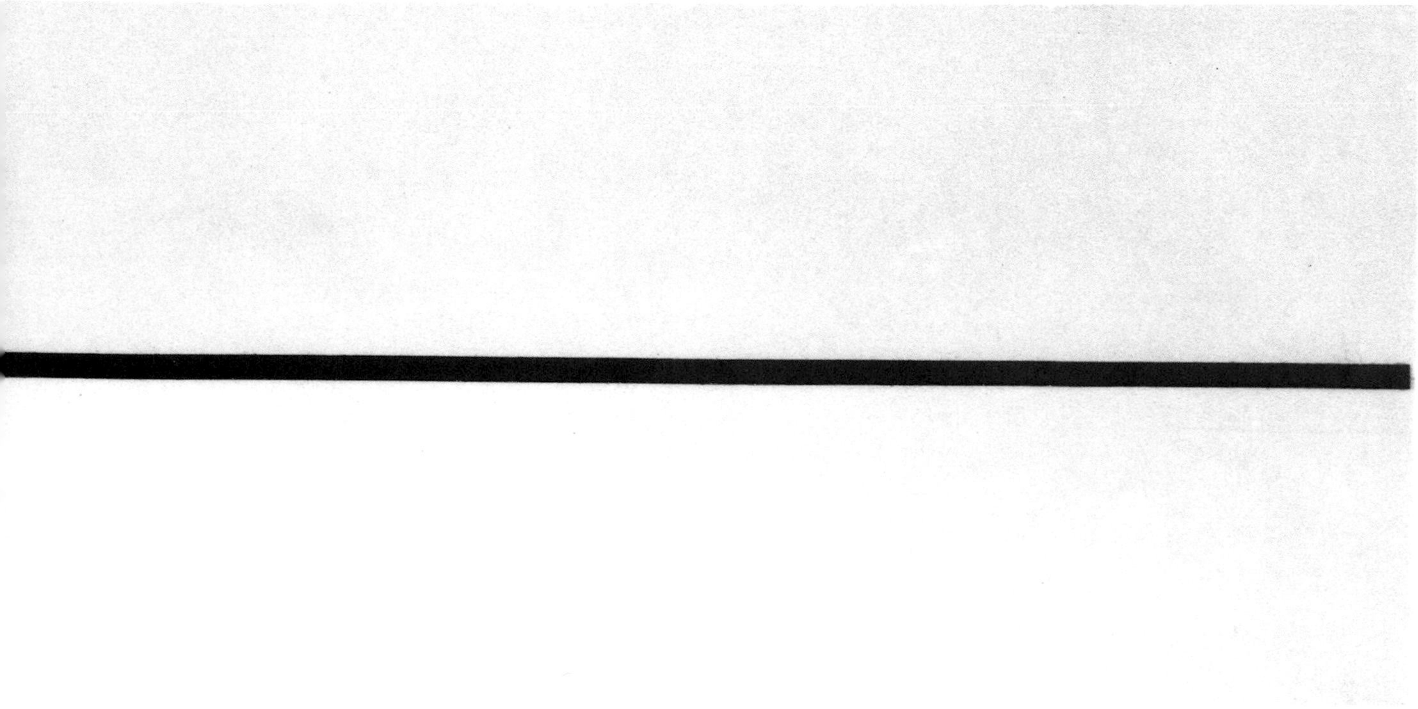

at Bennington College, then at Hunter College completing a masters of art history degree, Johanson made sculptural paintings and large-scale public works that seized the imagination of her contemporaries. Her huge minimalist canvases explored optical effects and the relationship between spectator and object, while Johanson's interests urged her into larger arenas. Her work expanded and moved outside. In 1968 she built a 1600-foot-long sculpture, *Stephen Long*, along an abandoned railroad track in upstate New York. The sculpture interacted with natural light, changing color in response to the landscape and movement of the sun. Her contemporaries recognized that her work had implications for architecture and landscape design.

James Fanning, editor at *House and Garden*, invited Johanson to design a garden for the magazine. While doing research for the commission, Johanson studied the history of garden design. She read books on agriculture, ecology, soil conservation, urban plan-

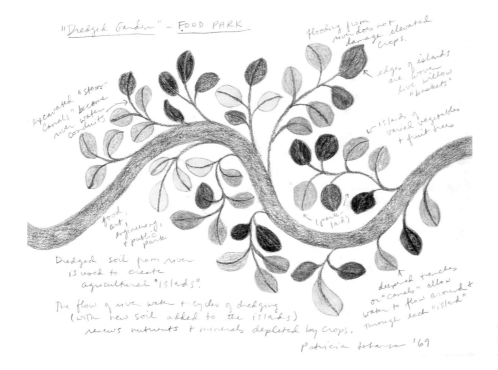

"Dredged Garden" – FOOD PARK

flooding from river does not damage elevated crops.

edges of islands are woven live willow "baskets"

islands of varied vegetables + fruit trees

excavated "stems" become "canals" + water river conduits

food, art, engineering, + public park

(park lot)

Dredged soil from river is used to create agricultural "islands".

The flow of river water + cycles of dredging (with new soil added to the islands) renews nutrients + minerals depleted by crops.

deepened trenches or "canals" allow water to flow around + through each "island"

Patricia Johanson '69

Dredged Garden: Food Park,
8 1/2" x 11", pencil and colored pencil,
1969

6

ning and highway engineering, and began to imagine how she could work as an artist in that context. She drew over a hundred sketches, including proposals for large-scale infrastructure projects, and she wrote a series of essays exploring her ideas. The drawing *Dredged Garden – Food Park* imagines a sculptural form combining flood control, river dredging and irrigation for agriculture. *Linked Gardens (Bobolink)* proposes a series of widespread parks built to provide food and shelter for migrating birds. *Regional Highway Garden: Nature Walk* envisions a sculpture that functions as highway crossing, park and ecological corridor. In a drawing titled *Garden-Cities: Aerial Highway* Johanson describes a city with a "continuous network of forested roofs" that absorb rainwater, and buildings that provide microhabitats for animals and plants. It eventu-

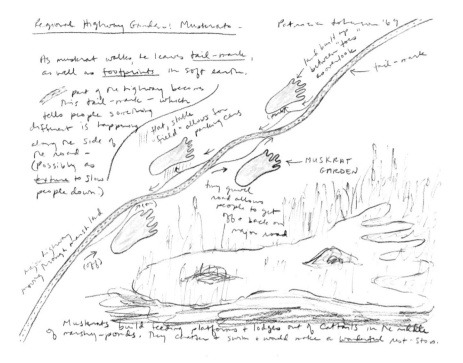

Regional Highway Gardens: Muskrats, 8½" x 11", pencil and colored pencil, 1969

ally became clear that *House and Garden* would never publish these visionary proposals. But the offer of a commission sparked a body of ideas and images that continue to inspire artists, environmentalists, landscape architects and urban planners.[1]

Johanson returned to building large-scale outdoor sculptures, while she pursued her vision by assembling credentials in engineering and architecture. She entered the Architecture Program at City College of New York, and worked for Mitchell-Giurgola, the well-known architectural firm. Then Johanson found she was pregnant. When she refused to have an abortion, the father, Eugene Goossen, suggested she raise their child on his remote property in Buskirk, 200 miles north of New York City. Though initially reluctant to leave the stimulating environment of galleries, work and friends, Johanson found she was happy in the isolated rural location. She loved being sur-

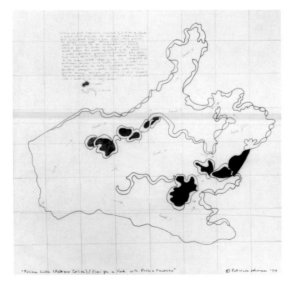

8

Above left: Feeding baby Alvar in Buskirk, 1974
(photo: Michael Marton)

Above right: *Dicot Leaf (Tulip Tree)*, drawing for a
sculptural landscape, 4 ⅞" x 4 ⅞", ink, c.1974

Left: *Foliose Lichen (Peltigera Collina)/Plan for a
Park with Pools and Fountains*, ink, 24" x 24", 1974

Facing page: *Color Landscape (Goeana Festiva)*,
30½" x 51", conté pencil and ink, 1981,
Gift of Isabel and William Berley, classes of 1947
and 1945, Courtesy of the Herbert F. Johnson
Museum of Art, Cornell University

rounded by natural seasons and cycles, quiet and solitude, the wonder of her infant son and an abundance of animals and plants. Small plants in the woods around her home caught her attention, and Johanson began her most important life-long dialogue – with nature. During the day, she made tiny drawings of plants while she watched her child. Late at night, when the baby was finally asleep, she would transform these tiny drawings into large-scale architectural projects.

People saw her plans and drawings in art galleries, and eventually she was invited to design and build her art as large-scale public projects. In the 1980's in Dallas and in

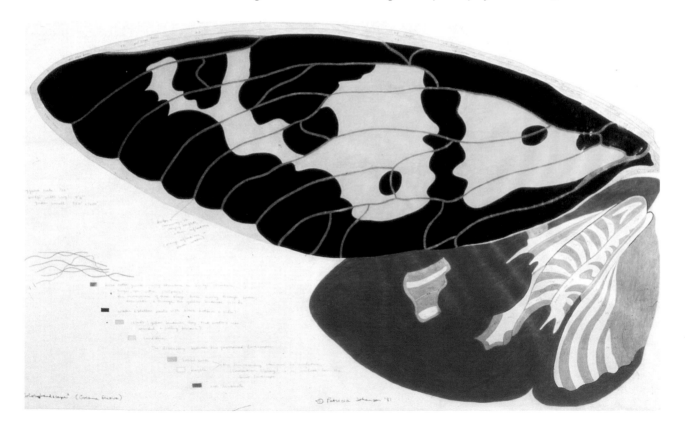

San Francisco she was able to prove that her ideas were sound by constructing gigantic environmental designs that functioned simultaneously as sculpture, park, habitat restoration and infrastructure. Then, at age forty-eight, Johanson was diagnosed with terminal cancer. While she mustered her creative resources to find a personal path to wellness, she began to envision art and survival in ever-more holistic terms. Her subsequent designs, including *Nairobi River Park* in Kenya, *Petaluma Wetlands Park* in California, and *The Rocky Marciano Trail* in Brockton, Massachusetts, cleanse water and create habitat for many species, while providing multiple economic and social benefits for human inhabitants. Johanson says that surviving cancer made her feel "fearless and invincible, ready to speak on global issues." [2]

As Johanson developed her hybrid art slowly and independently over four decades, she worked for many years in complete isolation, without ever knowing whether she would see her ideas constructed, or even viewed as serious proposals. She notes "many

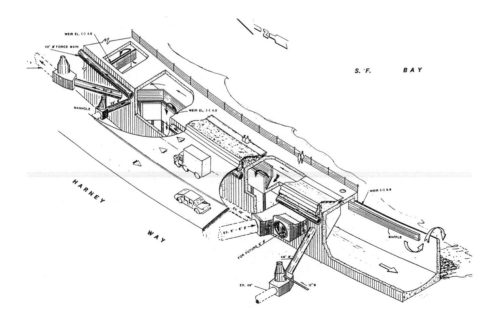

Left: *Endangered Garden*, San Francisco: sewer functions beneath baywalk, with highway (left) and San Francisco Bay

Facing page: *Endangered Garden: Site Plan*, Candlestick Cove, San Francisco, 22" x 32 ¾", 1988

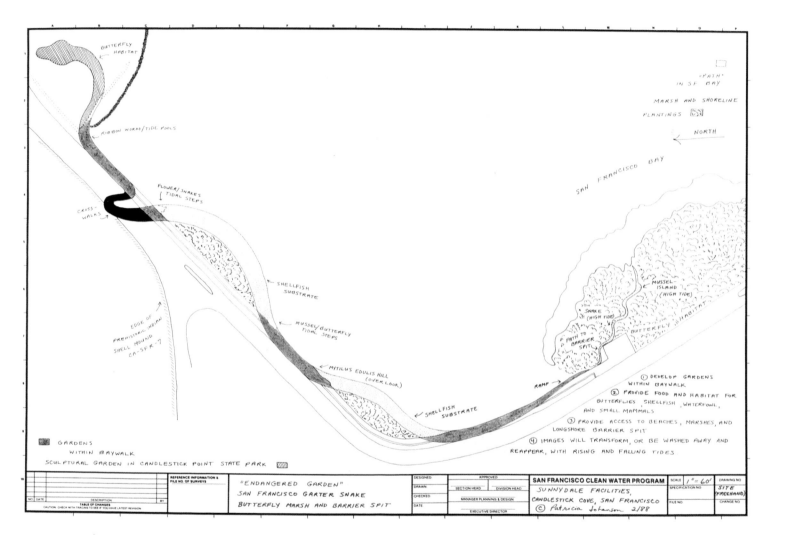

BUTTERFLY HABITAT

RIBBON WORM/TIDE POOLS

FLOWER/SNAKES
TIDAL STEPS

CROSS-
WALKS

EDGE OF
PREHISTORIC INDIAN
SHELL MOUND
CA-SFR-7

SHELLFISH
SUBSTRATE

MUSSEL/BUTTERFLY
TIDAL STEPS

MYTILUS EDULIS HILL
(OVERLOOK)

SHELLFISH
SUBSTRATE

"PATH"
IN SF BAY

MARSH AND SHORELINE
PLANTINGS

NORTH

SAN FRANCISCO BAY

MUSSEL
ISLAND
(HIGH TIDE)

SNAKE
(HIGH TIDE)

PATH TO
BARRIER
SPIT

BUTTERFLY HABITAT

RAMP

① DEVELOP GARDENS
WITHIN BAYWALK

② PROVIDE FOOD AND HABITAT FOR
BUTTERFLIES, SHELLFISH, WATERFOWL,
AND SMALL MAMMALS

③ PROVIDE ACCESS TO BEACHES, MARSHES, AND
LONGSHORE BARRIER SPIT

④ IMAGES WILL TRANSFORM, OR BE WASHED AWAY AND
REAPPEAR, WITH RISING AND FALLING TIDES

GARDENS
WITHIN BAYWALK

SCULPTURAL GARDEN IN CANDLESTICK POINT STATE PARK

REFERENCE INFORMATION &
FILE NO. OF SURVEYS

TABLE OF CHANGES
NO. DATE   DESCRIPTION   BY
CAUTION: CHECK WITH TRACING TO SEE IF YOU HAVE LATEST REVISION

"ENDANGERED GARDEN"
SAN FRANCISCO GARTER SNAKE
BUTTERFLY MARSH AND BARRIER SPIT

DESIGNED   APPROVED
DRAWN   SECTION HEAD   DIVISION HEAD
CHECKED   MANAGER PLANNING & DESIGN
DATE   EXECUTIVE DIRECTOR

SAN FRANCISCO CLEAN WATER PROGRAM   SCALE 1"= 60'   DRAWING NO

SUNNYDALE FACILITIES,   SPECIFICATION NO   SITE
CANDLESTICK COVE, SAN FRANCISCO   (FREEHAND)
© Patricia Johanson 2/88   FILE NO   CHANGE NO

Above: *Medusa Fountain (Rainbow Pools) Plan of Colors* (detail), 36" x 80", acrylic and ink, 1984

Facing page: Overview of *Fair Park Lagoon* from the Dallas Museum of Natural History

of the projects being constructed today were actually designed years ago and exhibited in art galleries, where they were discussed as 'visionary fantasies.' " Since her cancer diagnosis, Johanson has been even more concerned with creating model designs that can illuminate and inspire creative solutions, whether she sees them built or not.

"What I'm trying to do is take every project that I'm offered and figure out how I can best benefit not only local people and wildlife, but also how I can use that project as a model for the future. I want each design to say to people, 'This is how you can process your sewage and also provide all these other benefits. This is what you can do with your detention basins and highway shoulders that just collect trash.'"

Johanson points to large tracts of public land in the form of roads, powerlines, sewers and other infrastructure. She suggests that these woeful, derelict spaces could become interconnected living landscapes supporting wildlife and people.

"Beyond accomplishing any particular project, I always have goals that reach out to the whole world and its future. Small projects ask large questions, and point out that the world is of a piece. You can't do something in one place, whether it's positive or negative, without repercussions throughout the whole system. Each of my projects is a model for an inclusive, life-supporting, self-sustaining world."

Above: *South Ninth Street Corridor*, Salina, Kansas (detail), Railroad and Agriculture medians, 2001

Left: Patricia Johanson and Wang-Heng Chen at Jiang-Jia-Jie National Forest Park, China, 2004
(photo: Johanna Hallsten)

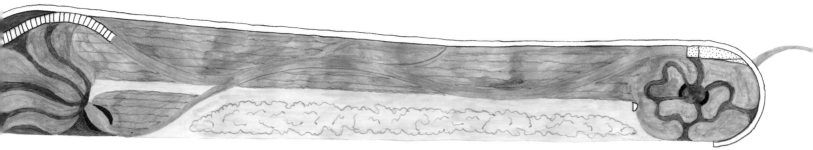

Johanson's art reclaims degraded environments and creates conditions that allow endangered species to survive. Children play in her designs. Animals, birds and bugs are there, not as captives, but because she has created nourishing, life-sustaining habitat. Sculptor Tony Smith, Johanson's lifelong friend and teacher at both Bennington and Hunter, told her one day in the 1960s, "There are many artists, but only one artist for any given time, and you are going to be that artist." According to Johanson, "Nothing needs to be wiped out. Opposites can be resolved, and 'problems' can add to the strength of the final result."[3] Using the structures of nature as a way of thinking, Johanson reconciles delicacy with strength, generosity with power and creativity with consequence.

NOTES:

1 Debra Bricker Balken was the first scholar to write extensively about the *House and Garden* drawings. See D. Bricker Balken, 1987, "The House and Garden Commission: Before and After" in *Patricia Johanson: Drawings and Models for Environmental Projects*, 1969-1986, Pittsfield, MA: The Berkshire Museum.

2 Unless a reference is supplied, quotations from Patricia Johanson are taken from conversations held in 1991, 2003 and 2004 and personal correspondence with the author 1989-2005. Some of this material has been previously published in Johanson, 1992.

3 Johanson, describing what she learned from building *Cyrus Field*, in handwritten manuscript titled "Biography written: 1984 – for Wonder Woman Award."

ART FOR THE LIVING WORLD

ART FOR THE LIVING WORLD

"The most important aspect of my art is in the parts I do *not* design," Johanson writes.[1] Rather than conceiving art as a series of objects erected in any landscape, Johanson's art invites people to encounter specific landscapes. A sense of place informs all of her projects. Johanson researches the unique history and ecology of each location. She consults with local naturalists and scientists, allowing the place to determine a project's shape and content. "I never design until I have discovered the meaning of the place. Each place has a unique set of conditions, and we need an intimate understanding of what it has been, is now, and will become in the future, in order to create a design that is more than a willful act," she says.

Modern life cleaves people from place. The ancient, informing experience of home regions has been replaced around the world by arbitrarily drawn borders and overlapping jurisdictions that bear no relationship with watersheds. Separated from the earth and one another, people lose their capacities for storytelling, finding medicines, tracking animals and talking to them. Nature is seen on TV or through a car window. The wilderness is a resource or a refuge, never a home. Johanson's projects ask what it would mean to *come home* to the places we inhabit. They function as maps that allow

Previous pages, left: *Pteris multifida*, nesting habitat

Right: *Saggitaria platyphylla*, *Shoreline Stabilization* (detail), 30" x 36", ink and pastel, 1982

Facing page: *Fair Park Lagoon*, lotus seeds eaten by wildlife

visitors to explore and discover a specific place in all its detail. Experiences within the artwork link inner and outer worlds, creating a homecoming to the site.

"The projects are designed to give people their place," says Johanson. "Each person finds their own meaning in it, and forms their own particular attachment to it. It's not the same from person to person. This is clear at *Fair Park Lagoon*. There are so many overlapping design strategies and entry points into the living landscape that almost everybody can find some connection to the place."

In 1978, Harry Parker, then director of the Dallas Museum of Art, saw Johanson's *Plant Drawings for Projects* at a New York gallery. He invited Johanson to envision a project for Fair Park Lagoon, a five-block-long body of water adjacent to the art museum and the Dallas Museum of Natural History. On Johanson's first site visit, the lagoon was a stagnant, dangerous eyesore in the middle of the city. The shoreline was eroding, and the water was murky. The parks department had been fertilizing the lawn. Every time it rained fertilizer would wash into the lagoon and cause an algal bloom. A green slime covered the water. There was no food chain; there were hardly any plants, animals or fish. "People had no experience of the water, except that a number of children had fallen in and drowned. The lagoon had become a danger and an obstruction," Johanson remembers.

She began to work with her own set of goals, developing a list of concerns that included creating a functioning ecosystem for a wide variety of plants and animals, controlling bank erosion, and creating paths so that people could safely cross the lagoon to visit the five museums surrounding it. She researched food and habitat requirements for different animals, realizing that specific plants would attract wildlife. The design had to solve a host of environmental problems, but also be acceptable to scientists, engineers and city planners.

The lagoon was planted with emergent vegetation that roots in shallow water, and further out with floating plants. Along the shore, Johanson planted tall grasses to provide shelter and food for small animals and birds. Sue Spaid notes that these bio-remediation aspects of Johanson's work may seem like common practice today, but they were totally experimental in 1981.[2] For the sculptural component of the project,

Saggitaria platyphylla, Dallas, Texas, 1981-1986
(photo: Albert Halff)

Johanson designed huge forms based on native plants and deployed them to solve a host of environmental problems. The Delta Duckpotato, *Saggitaria platyphylla*, and a Texas fern, *Pteris multifida*, were models for her enormous sculpture. She arranged roots, stems and leaves to stabilize the shoreline, create microhabitats and form paths, bridges, perches and overlooks. "Just before the project was dedicated, flocks of wild birds arrived. Different species of fish were introduced into an environment that could nurture them," Johanson remembers.

Walter Davis, acting director of the Dallas Museum of Natural History, worked with Johanson. "Today the lagoon teems with life," he writes. "Those who understand the

24

Previous pages, left: *Fair Park Lagoon*, gunite construction

Right: *Pteris multifida*, 225' x 112' x 12', gunite, plants and animals, 1981-1986

This page, top: *Saggitaria platyphylla*, water fluctuations.

Bottom: *Pteris multifida*, island

Fair Park Lagoon, Dallas, Texas, 1981-86. Lagoon: five city blocks with two sculptures *Saggitaria platyphylla*, 235' x 175' x 12', gunite; *Pteris multifida*, 225' x 112' x 12', gunite

Fair Park Lagoon in Dallas, designed in 1981, seeks a fusion of aesthetic form, functional infrastructure, and living ecology, where every element is part of a larger system whose parts are intricately related. The sculptural forms simultaneously control bank erosion, serve as paths and bridges over water and create microhabitats for a wide variety of plants, fish, turtles, and birds. The plants and animals, in turn, become living educational exhibits for the Dallas Museum of Natural History, improve water quality, and are consumed and perpetuated as members of the food chain. The entire five-block-long lagoon also serves as a municipal flood basin, thus familiar forms and paths of travel are frequently altered by fluctuating water levels. *Fair Park Lagoon* offers a functional and aesthetic framework in which ecological communities can evolve, life in all its messy complication can proliferate, and creation continues.

– Patricia Johanson,
February 24, 2000

intricacies of a functioning ecosystem find particular satisfaction here. A kingfisher visiting for the first time in decades signals that the water is clear enough for this master fisherman to spot minnows swimming beneath the surface. A pair of least bitterns, secretive inhabitants of the vegetative shoreline, moved in the first year [to nest successfully].... Ducks and turtles sun themselves on emergent parts of the sculpture, safe from predatory dogs and enthusiastic children. These plants and animals are not captives held for the enjoyment of human spectators. Most have chosen to live in the lagoon because it provides food and shelter for themselves and their offspring."[3]

Fair Park Lagoon is a nurturing, living world; it is also a popular and entertaining place. Children play alongside the insects, reptiles, birds and mammals that live there.

"Fair Park Lagoon is really a swamp – a raw, functioning ecology that people are normally afraid of," Johanson says. "The art project affords people access to this environment, so they can find out how wonderful a swamp really is. It's popular, not because people are overwhelmed by my sculpture. They're discovering a marvelous new world."

In 1996 and 1997, Jacqueline Zanoni de los Santos spent months at Fair Park Lagoon observing how people interact with the landscape in preparation for her master's thesis.[4] She describes how visitors enter the bowl-shaped site in which "each stretch, each curve, carries its own rhythm and its own discoveries." Once visitors are lured out over the water by the twisting paths, the sculpture disappears as their focus shifts to a dragonfly, a fairy shrimp, a spawning fish, or a water lily. The lagoon is a living landscape that is always changing. It contains all the myriad details that allow such landscapes to evolve and survive. Johanson trusts that most visitors to the lagoon "discover some vision of the design intelligence of nature, of which they are a part."

Johanson notes that confronting environmental issues means seeing past the conventional culture of nature. "I want to confront people with the world as it exists," she says. This means accepting the full scope of environmental problems. In the 1969 *House and Garden* drawings, Johanson envisioned "gardens" that would make environmental problems visible. She proposed creating a *Toxic Rainbow* by adding harmless, color-coded dyes to major water pollutants, so that "as harmful substances mixed with water, the specific poison, or mixed chemical cocktail is revealed." In another drawing, she suggests that a *Garden of Organized Killing / Soil Fertility* be located outside a slaughterhouse, where "The horror of organized killing is brought into the open in a public garden that enriches the soil with the blood of sacrificial victims. The stench of death is everywhere."

Seeing nature whole means acknowledging the smaller, less seductive parts in any environment, while challenging a visual culture that sees the natural world as a succession of poetic moments and cute animals. In a talk Johanson gave at a Dumbarton Oaks Symposium on Landscape Design, she said: "Body movement and gardens of unplanned experience turns spectators into participants, ensuring both a creative response and some consideration of forces that affect the landscape and our own lives. I have become increasingly interested in landscapes that confront us with the world as it exists, rather than those that think only in anthropocentric and aesthetic terms, which is ultimately not to our benefit."[5]

Johanson explored these ideas in her next large-scale public project at Candlestick Cove in San Francisco Bay. *Endangered Garden* is a sewer designed as a baywalk that allows public access to the waterfront while creating life-supporting habitat that permits the return of endangered species. The sculpture's unusual forms are based on the snake and worm – despised animals that people fear and destroy.

The opportunity to work on the sewer project came in 1987, when Jill Manton of the Arts Commission of San Francisco phoned and asked whether Johanson would be interested in working on a new pump station and sewage holding tank at Candlestick Cove under a "percent-for-art" ordinance. Manton had seen an exhibit of Johanson drawings that translated the patterns of butterflies into tidal landscapes.

At first, the Department of Public Works strongly resisted Johanson's participation, saying that the "percent-for-art" ordinance should not apply to sewers. Once her participation had finally been accepted, sewer engineers kept showing her drawings of a tiny building they had designed, saying, "you could do a nice design on the roof of this pumphouse." Johanson was adamant: "I made it clear that decorating the sewer wouldn't be very meaningful!" Finally it was agreed that Johanson would become the co-designer of the entire project. Johanson remembers that this only happened

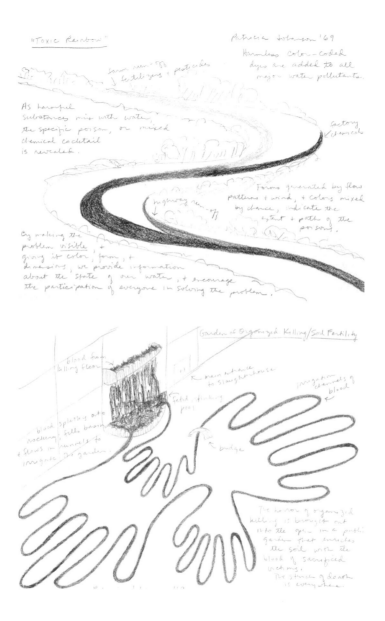

Top: *Toxic Rainbow*, 8 ½" x 11",
pencil and colored pencil, 1969

Bottom: *Garden of Organized
Killing/Soil Fertility*, 8 ½" x 11",
pencil and colored pencil, 1969

because "the Department of Public Works was desperate. Community groups had rejected its initial design, and there was a great deal of opposition to placing a sewer along San Francisco Bay. At the same time, the city was about to be sued by the Environmental Protection Agency for dumping raw sewage into the bay."

Johanson began with months of research on the site. She talked with experts on sedimentation, shellfish restoration and endangered species. She discovered that Ohlone Indians had inhabited this place for thousands of years. Candlestick Cove had also been home to a number of endangered species that had been pushed off the San Francisco peninsula as the city developed. Johanson wanted a design that would allow the return of some of these vanished plants and animals. She made endless sketches of "the minutiae of the site"[6] while trying to imagine how the sewer could become a public park that would bring people into contact with the natural environment.

Johanson decided the sewer should be buried. If its roof were made into a baywalk running for one-third of a mile around Candlestick Cove, this would allow people to walk alongside and down into the bay. "It was a very simple solution," she says. "Once we buried the sewer and established its roof as a public access baywalk, then it was just a matter of making the vertical connections between the sewer roof and the floor of the bay. In a way, that's what all my work is. It's about making the requisite connections."

Johanson found a unifying image for the project in the endangered San Francisco Garter Snake. "The San Francisco Garter Snake is a real snake, an endangered species, and very beautiful – red and aqua," she says. The snake was also perfect for creating habitat that would allow the return of endangered butterflies. Johanson explains: "This is a very windy area. By building the head of the snake as a high earth mound, I was able to create an area protected from wind, so that butterflies could fly there. Again, it's not just a matter of image. It's a matter of taking an image and using it to pursue the project's goals." The "Butterfly Meadow" behind the serpent's head has become a place where living butterflies thrive.

Johanson also recalls: "When I designed the project, people were really enthusiastic. They loved the idea that the public might actually be able to use one of these large infrastructure projects. For the first time, people were actually getting something for their money in addition to the functional facility they needed. The project had a lot of support. Many organizations wrote letters to the city saying what a visionary proposal this was and how much they wanted it." After a long public process, approvals and construction permits were finally obtained. But once community support was secured on the basis of Johanson's design, problems arose when the budget for art and landscaping was separated from funds for sewer construction. Johanson had to compromise her vision by using cheaper construction materials. Many of the specific features she had designed for the project were never built, including a songbird arbor and several tidal sculptures. The most devastating loss for Johanson was a shellfish substrate, which would have allowed people to wander onto the mudflats at low tide, while restoring shorebird food and shellfish habitat.

Johanson grieves for what *Endangered Garden* could have been, and remembers that when the project was eviscerated in the late 1980s she reacted with anger and outrage. She notes that working on such large-scale public projects, which require a constellation of multiple interest groups, agencies and funding sources, means one often has to face failure, postponement and even sabotage. But with the passage of time, Johanson has focused on the achievements of *Endangered Garden*. She is certain that the world at that one place is more livable and whole because of her involvement in the project.

Endangered Garden fills ecological gaps with food and habitat, making it possible for extirpated species to return to the site. Combining art with public recreation and enjoyment, the sculpture is also an educational opportunity. It presents visitors with a miniature world that integrates snake, bird, butterfly, worm, human and intertidal life. Author Barbara Matilsky notes: "The work fosters an environmental ethic regarding the value of even the smallest living things by making visible the tiniest animals of the bay."[7] In its images and again in its physical structures, *Endangered Garden* shows that art can support functioning ecosystems rather than perpetuate an ideal view of nature. In such ecosystems, small, unknown plants and animals are vitally important.

32

Endangered Garden (Sunnydale Facilities), San Francisco, 1987-97

The image for the project became the endangered San Francisco Garter Snake whose attenuated shape echoes the transport-storage sewer, and whose bright colors and varying patterns—stripe, scale, ventral plate, and "chains of mountains"—form the structural basis for individual gardens within the overall plan. Because the "snake" is so large, it is visible in its entirety only from several high points adjoining the site or from the air. It is also purposely directional and discontinuous, moving on and off the baywalk and "twisting its body" to shift patterns in order to create special stopping points, establish different rhythms, and focus attention on the life of the bay within this unwaveringly linear trail.

....The San Francisco Garter Snake mediates between human scale and the monolithic landforms that surround the site. Its head and neck, located in Candlestick Point State Recreation Area, were designed as twenty-foot high earthmounds that echo both San Bruno Mountain to the west, and the terminal recurve of the longshore barrier spit at the opposite end of the baywalk. This miniature "mountain range" creates windbreaks, sunning platforms, and shelter from predators for endangered butterflies. It is set within a planted meadow that provides nectar for the butterflies and specific host plants for their larvae. Many visitors take notice of the butterflies, caterpillars and other insects on the flowering plants. Surprisingly, a number of visitors to the meadow remark on the tiny "mountain range" of the snake's head, which aligns itself with San Bruno Mountain in the distance....

The coiled tail section of the sculpture leads to a high point that serves as a "box seat" for the action on the "stage" of the bay below. This erratic sculptural projection is often a gathering point for school groups.... It provides the grand ascendant overview, encompassing the sweep of the landscape, while its descending terraced counterpart, the "Ribbon Worm," steps down for a more intimate experience of life along the shore. Several worm loops fill with water, creating habitat pools within the sculpture. The steps provide access to a small beach, and the cove's continuous

but dynamic and shifting boundary where land and water meet....

The sculpted ribbon worm echoes the larger baywalk snake as well as the tiny living ribbon worm, Emplectonema gracile, found at the site in tangled masses among mussels and barnacles. Similar undulating forms, ripple marks, are formed by underwater currents and repeated incessantly underfoot. This fusion of form, function, and ecological system that I want the visitor to discover and its pervasiveness from microcosm to macrocosm often lie along a mucky path.

– Patricia Johanson, 2003

Previous pages, left: *Endangered Garden*, birds feeding on mudflats

Right: *Endangered Garden*, 500' x 400' Butterfly Meadow sheltered by 20' high earthmound (head of snake)

Opposite page top: *Endangered Garden*, San Francisco, "Ribbon Worm/Tidal Sculpture", 75' x 25' x 8', gunite, 1987-1995

Middle: Schoolchildren picnic on *Coiled Tail Overlook*

Bottom: *Endangered Garden*, serpentine ripplemarks on mudflats

Above: *Endangered Garden, Coiled Tail Overlook and Cantilevered Tail*, 22" x 34", acrylic and ink, 1989

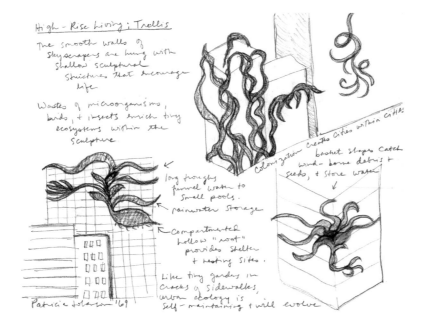

High-Rise Living: Trellises, 8½" x 11",
pencil and colored pencil, 1969

Changing the culture of nature to allow acknowledgement of its minute processes is a key aspect of Johanson's work.

Johanson designs for all of nature, including human nature, as she formulates an art that supports life, allows diversity, cleans air and water, and creates microhabitats. She sees it as vital that people not be left out of the culture of the wild. In San Francisco, opposition to her plans to build a shellfish substrate came not just from bureaucrats and budget cuts, but also from environmentalists, who wanted no human activity in the intertidal zone. They felt this area should be preserved for the benefit of wildlife. But Johanson sees this attitude as part of the problem. The shellfish substrate would have put something back into the environment to model her vision – that people can live with nature in a mutually beneficial way. Oyster beds were once prevalent in San Francisco Bay. They failed shortly after the intertidal zone became government property and Native Americans were prohibited from their traditional practice of har-

*Garden-Cities: (Brassica oleracea) –
Pattern of Urban and Rural Districts,
8½" x 11", pencil and colored pencil,
1969*

vesting the shellfish. Decades later, scientists came to understand something that the native people have said all along – annual harvesting prevented the oyster beds from silting over. Oysters suffocated in the muddy bay when they were isolated and "protected." "People are so afraid," Johanson says. "The preservationists always want such complete control that they diminish what they have. I have as much trouble with people who are narrow preservationists as I do with people who don't understand anything about ecological communities."

Johanson advocates for a new culture of nature that can reintegrate people with the non-human world. "People have a place in nature," she says. "They shouldn't be left out of the equation." Early *House and Garden* drawings envision cities interwoven with wilderness. In her 1969 essay, "Garden-Cities," she writes, "By interweaving man's constructs with the profuse phenomena of nature – water, geological formations, plants and animals in their natural habitats – it might be possible to shift away from a world

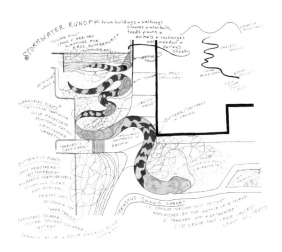

36

Sugar House Pedestrian Crossing,
Salt Lake City, Utah, 2003

The goal of the Sugar House Pedestrian Crossing is to create an accessible link across a major highway, completing an essential connection in Parley's Creek Trail. It is designed to reflect the natural and cultural history of this place (one of the first areas settled by the Mormons)– as well as enhance the contemporary biological corridor– all within the framework of human infrastructure. By using color and sculptural forms to create unique landmarks and a sense of the journey, typical engineering is transformed into a many-layered project that is aesthetic, ecological, educational and useful.

The project begins with a trailhead along Thirteenth Street East, overlooking Parley's Creek as it flows down from the mountains and the Bonneville Shoreline Trail. This overlook is formed by the rounded "bulb" of a "Sego Lily," with

"root hair" railing, perches and nesting shelves incorporated into the structure below. The green "stem" and slender "leaf" of the lily form descending paths that flow sculpturally within undulating topography, linking Sugar House Park and the pedestrian crossing to Parley's Creek Trail.

At the bottom of the hill, the entrance plaza– the "Sego Lily" flower– echoes the park's ornamental planter beds, and fits into its surrounding grassy bowl, a topographical dam engineered for flood control. These functional and sculptural berms surrounding the entrance to the highway crossing become a microcosm of both Sugar House Park as detention basin and the great Salt Lake Valley itself. Pedestrians are free to jog along the top of the dam, or wander the grassy slopes that form infinite "paths" leading down into the crossing.

.... Across the highway, storm water is harvested from the roof of an adjacent building and carried over the "ravine" to the top of a "Living Hill," where it flows through water features, feeds plants and animals, and recharges a wet meadow and Parley's Creek, which reappears from an underground culvert.

The wilder natural landscape of Hidden Hollow is echoed by emanations of a "rattlesnake," whose patterns transform into waterfalls, retaining walls, paving patterns, and a miniature "creek," all linked by food and habitat plantings for birds and butterflies. ... Colorful sculptural retaining walls hold the soil along a steep slope, while incorporating niches and crevices for wildlife.... Shallow pools near the wet meadow attract butterflies and hummingbirds, and are connected to the "Living Hill" by colorful paving patterns that suggest tiny insects, as well as monumental mountains within the body of the

"snake." Hidden Hollow is an urban treasure that, like the pedestrian crossing, provides safe passage for wildlife through the human landscape.

– Patricia Johanson, 2003, unpublished manuscript titled "Sugar House Pedestrian Crossing: Design Narrative."

Opposite page top: *First sketch for Sugar House Park: "Rose"*, 5¾" x 6", pencil, 2003, inspired by Brigham Young: "Mormons would make the desert bloom like a rose."

Bottom: *Sugar House Pedestrian Crossing: "Snow's Snake/Stormwater Runoff"*, 20" x 25", acrylic, ink and colored pencil, 2003

Right: *Sugar House Pedestrian Crossing: "Sego Lily"*, 28" x 15", acrylic, ink and colored pencil, 2003

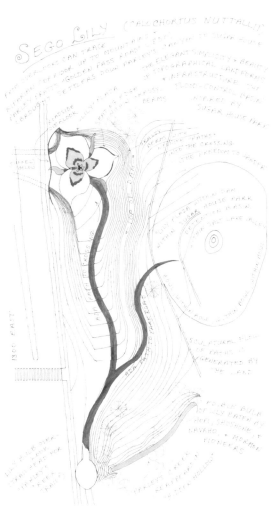

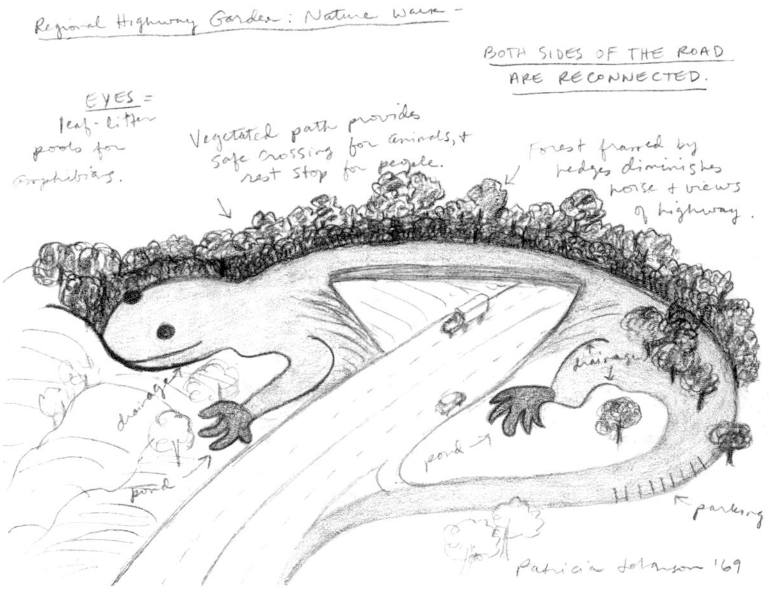
Regional Highway Garden : Nature Walk -
BOTH SIDES OF THE ROAD ARE RECONNECTED.
EYES = leaf-litter pools for amphibians.
Vegetated path provides safe crossing for animals, + rest stop for people.
Forest framed by hedges diminishes noise + views of highway.
drainage
drainage
pond
pond
parking
Patricia Johanson '69

Regional Highway Garden: Nature Walk, 8½" x 11", pencil and colored pencil, 1969

oriented to power and profit, to a world oriented to life." In plans and projects that interweave the intensely urban with the wild, Johanson argues with preservationists for designs that bring people together with nature. She wants public access to every part of her projects. Instead of conceiving of the wild as a space preserved outside ordinary experience, in beautiful parks that might be visited once in a lifetime, Johanson designs wilderness parks for the roof of a parking garage and featureless highway medians. Her art shows how the physical structures of contemporary human society can create space where wild nature can flourish, becoming part of the everyday reality of our lives.

In Salt Lake City, Utah, Johanson designed a pedestrian crossing for an eight-lane highway. She found in this 2003 project an opportunity to restore an historic ravine both as pedestrian crossing and biological corridor. Color and sculptural forms create unique landmarks and enhance a sense of the journey. A sculptural "Vertical Garden"

First sketch for *Parley's Creek Trail: "Salamander"*, 6" x 3½", colored pencil, 2003. The salamander lives along the creek in leaf litter.

below the highway affords habitat niches and planting pockets. Stormwater harvested from the roof of an adjacent building is carried overhead to the top of a "Living Hill," where it creates waterfalls, flows through water features, feeds plants and animals and recharges a wet meadow and a creek. The *Sugar House Pedestrian Crossing*[8] is designed to reflect both the natural and cultural history of the place. It creates a wildlife corridor within the framework of human infrastructure. A typical engineering problem – a pedestrian tunnel – is transformed into a multi-layered project that is functional, beautiful and ecological.

Johanson recently visited Fair Park Lagoon in Dallas, and was delighted to watch people experiencing art and nature within her designs. Reflecting on that experience, she says: "The ordinary is very important to me – that art is not on a pedestal, not hermetically sealed away, that animals and plants are not living behind bars or maintained in a perfect temperature-controlled environment. We tend to enshrine and protect our resources. Ultimately daily life is more important than a Sunday outing. It goes to the issue of how we really live. Do you have one good experience and then go back to a tedious existence? Or is your daily life enriched and enhanced?"

Johanson sets out a new vision for public land, where sewage treatment plants, highways, garbage dumps and other functional landscapes are designed as both art and habitat. As a child, she was deeply nourished by time spent playing in public parks designed by Frederick Law Olmsted (1822-1903). Like Olmsted, Johanson creates democratic meeting grounds where people from all social classes come to experience nature. Unlike Olmsted, Johanson brings ecological communities into her designs. Her democratic view includes birds, insects and microorganisms. "To me it's all equally important," she says, "the microscopic bacteria and the man who contributes a million dollars to the project."

Johanson's egalitarian ethos shapes both her art and life. She contrasts her life, which she describes as "so ordinary in many ways – filled with the daily struggles of having children, cooking meals, doing laundry," with the notion of artist as romantic genius that she learned as a student. "When I was a student you had to be a tormented alcoholic to be considered a real artist – the Jackson Pollock syndrome. I was taught that art posits hierarchies, starting with the idea that the artist is different from and superior to everyone else. The cultural object was ideal and perfect, destined for the museum or home of a wealthy collector. What I've been trying to do is dissolve the hierarchies and get everything on the same level – the art, the people, the plants, the soil, the water."

Johanson's democratic values make it vital that she not impose meaning, but rather, create spaces in which meaning can be discovered. She finds that when nature is brought into the work, its meanings resonate with every visitor's personal experience and unique interpretation. "Most people who see my work are never going to read about it," she says. "The majority of contemporary artists depend on a body of art history or criticism – some interpreter out there who will say what the work is about. The average person is very insecure when going into an art gallery to look at painting or sculpture. My work is the opposite. You don't need to read anything; you don't need a PhD in art history. All you need to do is come into contact with it – and whatever you think about it is valid. I'm not interested in telling people what they should think. I try to create situations where people can understand, through their own experience, how the world works."

Other artists have found it difficult to make space for their own creativity and vision while juggling the multiple, competing demands that come with working in the public realm. Between incorporating public input, assimilating information and research, and navigating approval processes, the art can get lost. Johanson insists the art is vital. She is an internationally renowned site planner and landscape designer, yet she always identifies first as an artist. Her ideas are rooted in an artist's palette of image, color, form, pattern, symbol and the relationship between spectator and object. She believes that art offers an experience that other forms of creativity do not. "By discovering an image, people can find things out for themselves, and it can be different for each person."

NOTES:

1 Johanson, 2000.

2 S. Spaid, 2002, *Ecovention: Current Art to Transform Ecologies*, Cincinnati: The Contemporary Arts Centre, p. 76.

3 W. Davis, January 24, 1992, letter to Johanson.

4 J. Zanoni de los Santos, 1997, *Tracing the Experiential Path: Large-Scale Sculpture by Patricia Johanson*, Master's Thesis, University of Oklahoma Graduate College, Norman, p. 23.

5 Johanson, 2000.

6 Johanson, 1988, typewritten document annotated by the artist, "written Feb. 1988, *Statement about Drawing* for Judy Van Wagner exhibit: '100 Drawings by Women,' published in: *Lines of Vision: Drawings by Contemporary Women*, by Judy K. Colloschan Van Wagner, Hudson Hills Press, NY, 1989."

7 B. Matilsky, 1992, *Fragile Ecologies: Artists' Interpretations and Solutions*, New York: Rizzoli International, p.56.

8 Johanson's design won the 2004 Envision Utah Grand Achievement Award for Planning and Design.

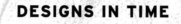
DESIGNS IN TIME

"Snake in the Grass for Philip Glass" - Pattern of Water

1. Trinket Snake
2. Burmese Rock Python (Indian Python)
3. Mangrove Snake
4. Old World Whipsnake
5. Ball Python
6. Emerald Tree Boa

© Patricia Johanson '95

All rights reserved, including all rights to reproduce the work.

Previous pages, left: *Stephen Long*, Buskirk, New York, 2' x 1600' x ½", acrylic on plywood, 1968

Right: *Underwater Sculpture/Reef/ Marine Habitat* (detail), 8½" x 11", pencil and colored pencil, 1969

Facing page· *Snake in the Grass for Philip Glass, Pattern of Water*, 42" x 69", acrylic, ink and gouache, 1985

WHEN 18-YEAR OLD PATRICIA JOHANSON ARRIVED AT BENNINGTON COLLEGE IN 1958, she intended to major in music. During high school, she was a devoted musician, a member of both the orchestra and marching band. She remembers "marching down the 50-yard line, forming images of trains while playing 'Chattanooga Choo-Choo'!" Laughing, she admits the influence of the marching band's democratic exploration of sound, pattern, time, space and public enthusiasm.

"When you think about what music is, it really is overlapping patterns. And I realize that is very much what I try to accomplish with my projects – a symphony of different voices." In Johanson's designs an overarching theme unfolds in time – supported by small moments, movements, solos, and minutiae that are key to the final result.

In 1985, Johanson created a design for an urban park called *Snake in the Grass for Philip Glass*. The project honored Johanson's friend, the well-known composer, with overlapping patterns inside a composition that unfolds in time and space. When snow falls on the project, covering the colors, a sculptural flower becomes visible. When the snow melts, decorative flat patterns of snakes are revealed. Johanson explains: "Creating overlapping patterns within the same composition is an idea I use again and again in different ways. Because these patterns unfold in time, you may need to reach

Snake in the Grass for Philip Glass, Plan of Park Features, 42" x 69", ink, pastel and charcoal, 1985

46

the end of the composition before you see how the beginning is connected. With accumulating knowledge, the patterns keep shifting, so you are putting it together in your mind as you go – very much as you experience music."

Visitors to Johanson's projects are invited to use memory, attention, imagination, and research to see the images and understand the artist's intent. "The person inside the work needs to make the requisite connections. It is not as though the artist is doing everything," Johanson says. In addition to the artist's voice, she hopes to make spaces in which many voices, both inside and outside the work, have a chance to speak and be heard. "I've always been very interested in symphony orchestras, where one voice comes to the fore and then recedes into the background," she says. Johanson describes the meaning of her works as consisting in "whatever is coming to the fore at any given moment. For an artist like me, that would be whatever people notice, whatever it is that attracts their interest." The works invite visitors into an "unfolding relationship" with form and content. Writing of her San Francisco project *Endangered*

Garden, Johanson says, "This fusion of form, function, and ecological system that I want the visitor to discover, and its pervasiveness from microcosm to macrocosm, often lies along a mucky path. I believe such unfolding relationships require individual wanderings, the considered pause, and knowledge acquired over time...."[1]

Johanson has always been interested in creating environments rather than objects. While a student at Bennington in 1960, Johanson conceived and constructed a *Color Room*.

"For a class project I painted paper different colors – orange, green and black – and draped an entire room. With the light coming through the paper, it was as if you had walked into a painting. I put a black and green object in the center of the room, whose shapes related to those of the walls and sloping ceiling." Her studio teachers, Paul Feeley and Tony Smith, were excited by the work. Other faculty came to see it, as did artists Kenneth Noland and David Smith. While they all found the young student's work deeply interesting, the college administration was less enthusiastic. They considered the draped paper a fire hazard, and moved immediately to tear it down. Johanson became briefly embroiled in a conflict that foreshadowed her later projects, as she tried to protect the work from destruction.

"I was trying to take painting beyond the object and make it into an environment – an environment that people would experience in their own space, at their own pace. They were no longer just looking at something. They were participating in the process." During her time at Bennington, Johanson constructed several of these *Color Rooms* – her first experiments with designs that unfold in time.

By creating environments into which viewers could walk, while attending to unfolding relationships and shifting images, Johanson addressed her early dissatisfaction with the confines of pictorial objects and aesthetic experience. In one of the *Notebooks* she kept at Bennington, she wrote: "As you drive along a winding road, you never know what lies around the bend. Possibly art should be like this. (Compare the all-at-onceness of the usual painting. It is all there in front of you at any given moment for you to contemplate... or the relatively short time it takes to walk around even a large piece of

48

Color Room, Bennington College, Bennington, Vermont, 1960

Color Room dealt with color in space, and also with three-dimensional positive-negative space. It consisted of an over life-size irregularly faceted green and black "object," and an equally irregularly faceted orange "space": the "room" (Paul Feeley's office) with its walls, floor, and sloping roof completely covered with orange paper. Once having entered, you were outside part of the sculpture, inside the rest. Together they united to form a non-decorative color-space in which different "compositions" could be created by moving through the work.

– Patricia Johanson, 1973

traditional sculpture). With the road, it takes a long time to know the configuration – and possibly you never know."[2]

A few years later, Johanson began to incorporate nature into her work. Sculptor David Smith challenged her with the statement that sculpture could not be horizontal. In response, Johanson built *William Rush* as a 200-foot-long horizontal line. The sculpture was fabricated from a structural tee (an I-beam, cut in half) painted with red lead, and laid into an open clearing. "Immediately debris from the trees fell on the sculpture in different patterns. You would find a grasshopper, a frog or a snake sitting there," Johanson remembers. While others wanted to clean and preserve the work, Johanson was thrilled by the interaction of nature with the sculpture. She began to explore the possibility of creating a living art that would grow and change in time, shaped and enhanced by the natural world, instead of an art that had to be protected and maintained in an ideal state. The patterns and processes of nature – transitory effects of light, weather and seasons, the processes of growth and decay – became integral to her designs.

In 1968, Johanson's 1600-foot-long sculpture *Stephen Long* changed color in response to natural light. In the 1969 *House and Garden* drawings she created "Illusory Gardens....to capture fleeting effects of natural color, light and weather...." In a drawing titled *Walking Through the Sky* she suggests a garden made with sections of mirror, separated by narrow paths, to reflect the ever-changing moods of the sky. Johanson conceived of working with tides for the first time in the *House and Garden* drawings. She has explored this possibility many times throughout her career, for example, in the *Tidal Color Garden* (1982), a design for a park in an intertidal area. Johanson explains that this garden was conceived as "both topographical and sculptural, so that spatial relations, combined with color, would produce an ever-changing landscape of 'painted compositions' as visitors walked through it." This series of drawings was shown in 1984 at the Philippe Bonnafont Gallery in San Francisco where Public Art Administrator Jill Manton saw it. Years later, Manton asked Johanson to work on the sewer project in Candlestick Cove.

William Rush, Buskirk, New York, 8" x 200' x ¼," steel painted with red lead, 1966

Stephen Long, Buskirk, New York, 24" x 1600' x ½" acrylic on plywood, 1968

A fascination with Monet's "series paintings," and the idea of the optical mixture of colors led me to study the structure of the eye and the brain and the color theories of Chevreul. In England I had been affected by the way Stonehenge worked with nature, acting as an organizing and recording device for transient, but predictable, natural events.

And Leonardo had made it clear that color is partly determined by the amount of atmosphere that intervenes between the object and the eye of the observer. Out of doors where the "quality" of the atmosphere also changes ("weather") the effect on color is even more dramatic. All of these considerations led to my first two pieces of sculpture:

William Rush, two hundred feet long and painted a single color (red lead) functions almost like a piece of the landscape – continually reflecting the changes going

on around it. *Stephen Long*, sixteen hundred feet long and painted red, yellow, and blue, was more of a color experiment. At times the entire spectrum was visible due to optical mixing along the borders, and the painted colors were constantly in flux due to changes in the color of natural light. At sunset, for example, when red light was falling on the sculpture the blue stripe turned to violet; the yellow stripe turned to orange.

– Patricia Johanson, 1973

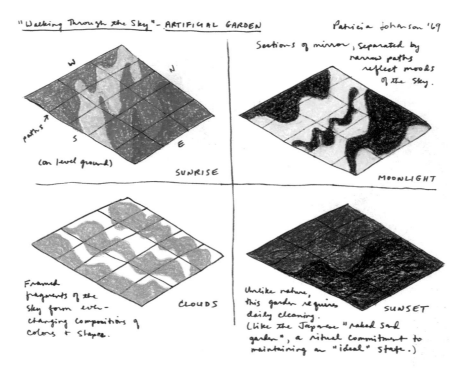

"Walking Through the Sky" – ARTIFICIAL GARDEN   Patricia Johanson '69

Sections of mirror, separated by narrow paths reflect moods of the sky.

W
N
paths
S
E
(on level ground)

SUNRISE

MOONLIGHT

Framed fragments of the sky form ever-changing compositions of colors + shapes.

CLOUDS

Unlike nature, this garden requires daily cleaning. (Like the Japanese "raked sand garden", a ritual commitment to maintaining an "ideal" state.)

SUNSET

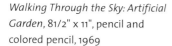

Walking Through the Sky: Artificial Garden, 8 1/2" x 11", pencil and colored pencil, 1969

"Everything is in constant motion, including us, and so we will see things with different eyes and find different meanings within the same work at different times in our lives," says Johanson. "Many of the ideas are fairly simple, dealing with the seasons, changes in the weather, tidal cycles, patterns of sunlight, shadow and darkness, and how this affects what we see. I like the idea that nothing is ever 'lost' but simply departs, and then returns on its own schedule – not ours ... like the tides. I try to design so that the flow of nature is made manifest."

Envisioning an art that incorporates transformations and interactions ran counter to all Johanson's training. She explains: "When I was first studying art, people used to say 'if it can be changed in any way, then it's not art.' There is an idea of art as a series of perfect, ideal objects. Parallel to that is the idea that artists are like gods, divine cre-

52

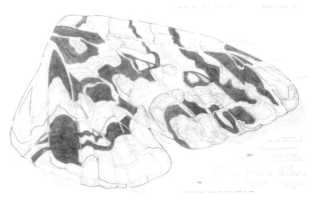

ators. Figures like Michelangelo were always invoked. As a female art student, I wondered, 'How can I ever be Michelangelo?' Ultimately, my answer was – 'Why try?'"

Instead of creating art – or parks – that must always be maintained, Johanson designs living landscapes that grow and evolve. "We are so unwilling, as artists, to let anything interfere with our grand vision. But anything that's alive has its own set of patterns and needs, and it's important not to expunge that in the process of creating our ideal works," she says. Johanson notes that the materials she uses must be carefully chosen so that they are enhanced, rather than destroyed, by the actions of nature on the project. She says unequivocally: "the important thing is not my sculpture, but what happens to it."

For Johanson, relinquishing control of her art is analogous to motherhood. "Motherhood taught me that the role of the creator, while important, is limited. You are heading into a long process. This is very different from what I was taught in art school– that you aim for perfection; your genius is recognized; and your work will be preserved by a grateful world forever. For me, incorporating unplanned experiences makes the work richer."

Johanson relinquishes control of her work not just to nature, but also to budgets and community processes. "When you are dealing with a scrap of paper, you can put down anything you want," she says. "It's your own personal work; there are no consequences in the real world. With the projects I design now, it's all consequences in the real world. There are real budgets. There are real sites. There are real community aspirations. There are real functional problems, and everything keeps changing as we proceed." She admits to terrible compromises on every project she has ever done, and cautions that without such compromises, artists may wind up with nothing at all. "The reality of large public projects is you never get what you want, but by being part of a creative process you are able to have some positive impact on the final result, and what's passed on to future generations."

Incorporating nature whole into the work can mean accepting risk and confronting fear. Johanson's living art invites us to encounter nature in its entirety. "In order to have a complete ecosystem, you also have to incorporate the parts you don't like. You can't

Opposite page: *Tidal Color Garden (Arachnis dilecta)*, each 36" x 57", acrylic, ink and pastel, 1982

Top left: *Low Tide*: all sculptural features and colors are revealed

Top right: *Flood Tide*: as water flows into the garden, steps become waterfalls, paths become streams, and high points become islands

Bottom left: *High Tide*: a network of causeways are linked by veins that have become bridges

Bottom right: *Plan* showing park features

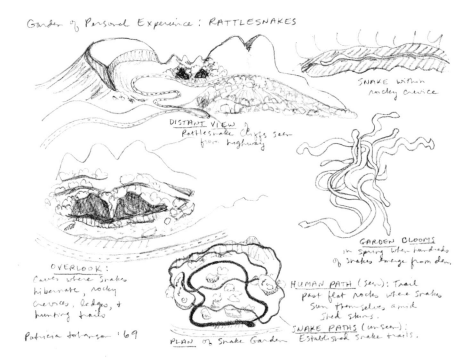

54

Left: *Garden of Personal Experience: Rattlesnakes*, 8½" x 11", pencil and colored pencil, 1969

Above: Snake explores *Cyrus Field* (photo: Gerrit Goossen)

change everything to make it conform to your own needs and desires, or to provide total human safety and security," she says. Excessive fearfulness results in sanitized museums where natural specimens are pinned to a wall. Johanson notes: "I would never design a dangerous public park; safety is always a primary concern. But people are threatened and impoverished by the relentless conversion of every scrap of territory for their own limited and temporary uses and by public landscapes that have been emasculated by legal departments and maintenance considerations."[3]

Johanson uses the perception of danger as a design element in her hypothetical *House and Garden* designs, like *Ocean Water Gardens* (1969), in which floating walkways and islands extend the public recreational area of a narrow beach by providing various levels of protected swimming and ocean walks. Johanson writes of this drawing: "These heaving, swaying paths over water – 'living' and 'unstable' – bring people far out into the ocean, isolating them within a powerful realm that is visually monolithic, yet alive and unpredictable. Floating walkways transmit the rhythmic beat, gentle surge, or even violence of the water underfoot, and within the deepest lagoon people can swim with fish and other ocean creatures that are attracted by the structure's underwater reefs." In a related project, *Underwater Sculpture/Reef/Marine Habitat* (1969), swimming is the form of locomotion through which visitors experience the project. At *Fair Park Lagoon*, the design – with its highly unusual, curving shapes – forces people to "slow down and watch their step, making them more attentive to their surroundings." Johanson writes: "Initially the sense that these are illogical, unpredictable forms, and perhaps even dangerous configurations, causes a constant referencing of one's body to the landscape, and a mental alertness lest a threat might appear. Regular visitors, on the other hand, know that this is a benign landscape, and seem to come seeking solace from the pressures of urban life."[4]

Johanson cautions that our view of nature cannot become whole if we go on trying to eliminate everything we fear. "We can't just have the 'good' parts without the parts that are less appealing to human beings. You need the whole system," she says. Her *Park for an Amazon Rainforest* is carefully designed to provide maximum safety for visitors. At the same time, this concept for a park at Obidos on the Amazon River brings visitors into an environment where there are venomous snakes and other dangerous creatures. Park visitors walk up into the rainforest, through a vast range of overlapping microhabitats, by means of a huge organic sculpture rising above the treetops. "This is a place of details and consequences, requiring careful consideration of where you stop, where you step, and where you put your hands," she comments. One of the goals of the project is to force people to move through an alien environment and confront their fears. Johanson notes that the relatively tiny scale of the human visitor, the height of the structure, and its perceived (but not actual) instability guarantee a respectful and carefully considered pace.

Johanson was one of a hundred international artists invited by the Brazilian government to attend the 1992 Earth Summit,[5] and she was asked to create a project for the Amazon rainforest. Her design for the park at Obidos translates a small bromeliad into a sculpture that rises 150 feet into the air and covers an area as big as a football field. Within the basic architectural structure, numerous microhabitats are created. As visitors ascend the sculpture, they experience the vertical stratification of the rainforest, with different life forms occurring at each level. Johanson imagines the sculpture would become encrusted with plants and colonized by innumerable species. The park is designed to allow visitors to journey through the rainforest ecosystem, seeing plants, animals, and ecological processes that are normally not visible. According to Johanson: "You start on the ground with caiman and capybara (the world's largest rodent), leaf-cutter ants, tarantulas, huge iguanas and many reptiles. Higher in the trees you encounter brightly-colored poison-dart frogs, and morpho butterflies – large, iridescent, blue-violet creatures that contrast with many smaller, brightly-patterned and camouflaged insects. Throughout the forest, orchids, bromeliads, hanging vines, and a cornucopia of fruits and nuts festoon flowering trees. Soon troops of monkeys appear. They are very inquisitive. If you've picked up some seeds or leaves, they will jump right onto your shoulder and pry your fingers open to capture the prize. Near the summit, colonies of oropendolas create woven-basket nests. Harpy eagles, macaws and sloths also live in the canopy." The design provides multiple paths and stopping points. It addresses the issue of deforestation through engaging visitors in an intimate experience of the ecosystem's intricacies, while providing an economic base for local residents.

When Johanson's drawings were first exhibited in Brazil, people immediately understood and embraced the project. Plans were made to build the park. From 1992 to the present, *Park for the Amazon Rainforest* has weathered several changes of government. "I think by the time they were on the third president, the government gave me the land," she recalls. "So I now have the deed to the land, and approvals from all

Facing page: *Park for a Rainforest (Tillandsia Streptocarpa): The Vertical Garden*, 34¾" x 50", ink, charcoal and colored pencil, 1992. This plan was exhibited at the Earth Summit in Rio de Janeiro, which led to the commission.

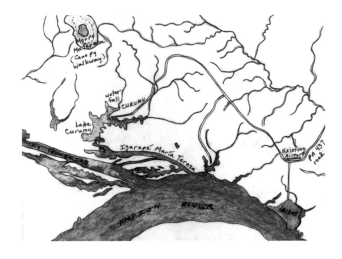

58

Clockwise, from top left: *Park for a Rainforest: Site Plan*, overall plan of Amazon journey, Obidos, Brazil, 7¾" x 9¾", ink and colored pencil, 1992; patterns of land and water during rainy season, Amazon River near Obidos; burned rainforest adjoining Amazon Rainforest Park site; Patricia Johanson at canopy walkway site, 1997 (photo: Nathaniel Goossen)

Facing page: View over Igarape Maria Teresa from canopy walkway site

The *Park for the Amazon Rainforest* forces us to move through an alien environment and confront our fears. The culminating experience is an exploration of forest stratification by means of a huge organic sculpture interwoven with a vast range of overlapping microhabitats. The plan of the walkways, which rise one hundred and fifty feet above the trees, is based on the leaves, flower stalk, and aerial roots of a bromeliad, *Tillandsia streptocarpa*, found at the site. The design strategy of the plant—a central column surrounded by long, narrow, cantilevered leaves—is translated into slender ramps, seating, and viewing platforms, providing access to every level of the rainforest ....

This is not a stroll garden. I go beyond style, entertainment, and connoisseurship to an earlier period of humankind when physical engagement and an accurate assessment of the landscape were necessary for survival. Moving through the rainforest strata places visitors within the beautiful but unfamiliar world of predatory insects, lianas, orchids, tree-snakes, poison frogs, iridescent morpho butterflies, algae-covered sloths, brilliantly colored macaws, aggressive troops of monkeys, and the harpy eagles that eat them. As they proceed, visitors are like birds who see the same territory unfold from different vantage points. In the process, they may learn that survival in such a landscape depends on vigilance and an intuitive understanding of context. They pause to rest but also to take in the information the landscape provides. Uncivilized gardens require creative negotiation and may engender in humans the same freeze-or-flight mechanisms of other species. Our relatively tiny scale, the height of the walkway, and its perceived, though not actual instability guarantee a carefully considered pace. The *Park for the Amazon Rainforest* encourages visitors to discover the dynamic flow of processes and develop their own dialogue with the endless complexity of the natural world.

– Patricia Johanson, 2003

the government agencies. The project was about to be built when my husband died, and it had to be put on hold once more."

Johanson's experience in the Amazon exemplifies another way in which her projects unfold in time. The large public projects take many years to complete, requiring the artist's patience, stamina and willingness to compromise. Only a small percentage of Johanson's designs have actually been constructed. The unbuilt projects, and the body of ideas she has created throughout her life, are a legacy for future generations.

NOTES:

1 Johanson, 2000

2 c. 1958, quoted by Johanson in a letter to Eleanor Munro, July 1, 1977, private papers.

3 Johanson, 2003, p. 99, n. 13

4 Johanson, 2000

5 The United Nations Conference on Environment and Development, held in Rio de Janeiro.

Facing page: *Park for the Amazon Rainforest*, model, 41½" x 29" x 10¼", 1992

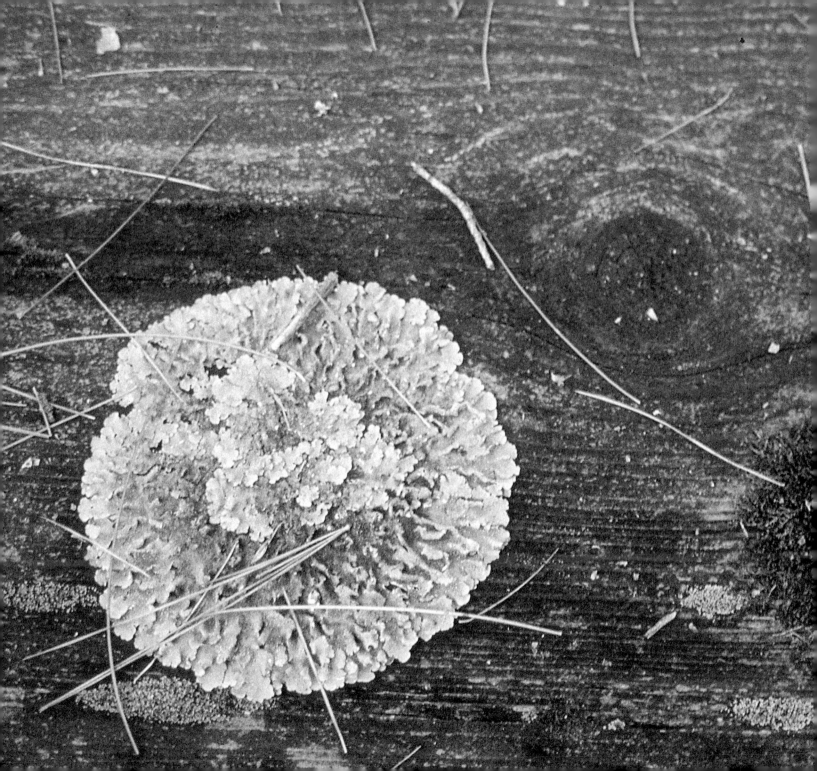

FRAMING THE WORLD AS A WORK OF ART

FRAMING THE WORLD AS A WORK OF ART

Previous pages, left: Lichens and moss growing on *Cyrus Field*

Right: *City of Brockton, Massachusetts: Brockton Village and Rocky Marciano Trail*, acrylic and ink on printed plan, 41" x 38", 1998

Facing page: *Cyrus Field-redwood*, Buskirk, New York, 12" x 2600' x 2", 1970. The redwood sculpture is often camouflaged by leaves and pine needles, as forest floor and sculpture become one. (Photo: Nathan Farb)

A WEATHERED MAZE OF MARBLE, REDWOOD AND CEMENT BLOCK WINDS THROUGH THE WOODS for over three miles near Johanson's home in Buskirk, New York. As visitors walk along the sculpture, they journey through forest ecosystems. The lines of *Cyrus Field* frame the natural world. Shortly after constructing the project in the early 1970's, Johanson wrote of her intentions, "*Cyrus Field* preserves its woodland setting in toto, yet restructures the experience of this setting by mediating between human scale and the vastness of nature. By incorporating the world around it, it transforms the woods into an almost infinite series of ever-changing compositions.... All become part of the work of art. The 'sculpture' simply provides a framework that gives the woods form and shape, making them visible and explicit, and giving the viewer an orientation to this world."[1]

The first section, made of marble, was constructed in 1970 with the help of a Guggenheim grant. Johanson says: "It was amazing to me what happened. On paper, the design is a simple geometric configuration, composed of identical components. On the ground, each line took on the life of the forest. It echoed flat or rolling topography and minute ecological changes as it moved through groves of birch and maple trees. The marble reflects everything that's going on around it – shadows, patterns of growth

Cyrus Field, Buskirk, New York, 1970, marble: 16" x 1200' x 4,"redwood: 12" x 2600' x 2," cement block: 8" x 3200' x 4"

Because it works with nature, both ecologically and aesthetically, *Cyrus Field* is self-maintaining and constantly changes with the seasons. I think it has some of the mystery of the remains of

Mayan cities that suddenly appear in the middle of the jungle– and like them will be subject to nature's encroachments, gradually being absorbed by the surroundings. Because they offer evidence of the hand of man, these pieces confer a meaning on the landscape that distinguishes it from all similar landscapes.

The marble piece is classical and serene– in plan a sub-divided square, two hundred feet on a side– its white lines creating a three-dimensional grid with the white birch trees. Like the Japanese "seasonal garden" it undergoes radical changes of color, mood, and texture: white on luxuriant green (summer); white on

bright yellow, then red, then brown maple leaves (fall); white on soft white (winter); white on decaying brown, then frail green (spring).

The redwood part is a triangular maze winding through a very dark and dense pine forest. Its center coincides with a small natural clearing– the only point at which sky is visible overhead and sunlight enters the woods. Because of its large size and the difficulty of the terrain only small fragments of the piece can be seen at a time, and the redwood blends with the carpet of red pine needles so that some sections are virtually invisible.

For a long time I had been fascinated with what things "are" as opposed to the way they are perceived, and I had begun to design some things that were impossible even to "figure out" because of their vast size and complex and unpredictable configurations. In thinking about possible subjects for the cement block section I remembered the decorative carvings in King's College Chapel: intertwined initials– HR, HA, AB– donated by Henry VIII in the hope of obtaining church approval for his marriage to Anne Boleyn. There was something personal, transient, and touching about the situation, and the straight lines and sweeping curves of the letters were both flexible and formally beautiful. I decided to substitute the initials of three friends. Later on I learned about the Nazca drawings in Peru – figurative, but so large that they are seen as abstract.

– Patricia Johanson, 1973

Facing page: *Cyrus Field-cement block*

Above left: Each 350-pound marble slab was hand carried into the forest by Johanson and her crew

Right: Patricia Johanson and Tony Smith looking at *Cyrus Field*, 1970

Left: *Cyrus Field-marble*, Buskirk, New York, 16" x 1200' x 4", 1970

Facing page left: *Cyrus Field-cement block*, scale plan showing intertwined initials of three friends: Patricia Johanson, Tony Smith and Eugene Goossen, 12½" x 8", ink on graph paper, 1970

Right: Nature is reflected on the marble in shadows, leaves, and leaf imprints

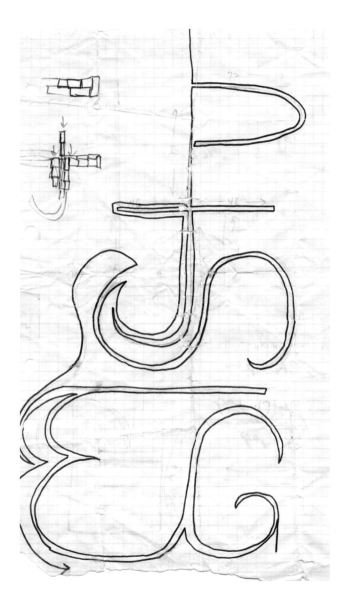

and decay, weather and seasons. In autumn a sea of fallen leaves dominates the sculpture – yellow, red, purple, then brown. The piece gets covered in snow, moves through patterns of melting ice, and in spring, a fragile green world again predominates. When you look at *Cyrus Field*, you see nature. Yet without the sculpture, you might not notice the various ecologies. The lines frame the natural world. They mediate between human and nature, without distorting or displacing anything. All the plants and animals are still there, and they even make use of the project. Snakes sun themselves on the marble; chipmunks live under the redwood, and small mammals tunnel along the edges of the cement block."

Building *Cyrus Field* was enormously important to the evolution of Johanson's work. She describes it as "the laboratory in which I evolved – where I learned what I wanted to do, and found out what was possible." She learned that by using line as a compositional device, she could "incorporate nature intact, without displacing or annihilating anything." Although the project is huge, it created no waste and did no harm to the environment.

"I realized that art could create large-scale order and poetry within which life could flourish," Johanson says. *Cyrus Field* has not had a large human audience, but it has been tremendously important to me."

In *Cyrus Field*, Johanson uses the line as a compositional strategy for creating "non-intrusive, interwoven structures" that frame functioning ecosystems. The art invites visitors to explore the world, while creating spaces in which nature can flourish. Describing this approach for Harvard's Dumbarton Oaks, Johanson writes: "My solution as a designer is painfully simple. Most of my plans simply frame intact or recreated ecosystems, appropriating wind, waves, and weather, all the transitory and elusive effects of color, light, seasons, and migratory cycles, and the passions and tragedies of countless plant and animal lives, as well as the deeper meanings that elude us. Thus the ceaseless movements of nature – the patterns and processes of life itself – become an integral part of the design."[2]

In Western cultural tradition, art depicts and displaces nature. Johanson tells the story of a childhood experience that predicts her different approach to the world. "One day when I was very little, I caught a butterfly. I was holding it carefully – but of course it was fluttering, trying to get away. A woman asked me, 'Little girl, what are you going to do with that butterfly?' I said, 'I'm going to take it home and make a drawing of it.' She warned me that if I did that, the butterfly would die. Somehow – I didn't want to, but I let it go. I watched it flutter away. And that's really the choice we have. Do we want to kill it and keep it for our own purposes, or do we want to let it live? I decided that I wanted to let it live. I have always chosen life over this death image of art. I love art – but I think sometimes it asks too much."

With *Cyrus Field*, Johanson creates an art that frames nature, allowing it to live. This simple concept required a huge shift in thinking. In the face of centuries of cultural tradition venerating unique art objects created by people of genius, Johanson developed an art that could shift viewers' attention from the created object to the world unfolding inside and around it. She muses: "Most artists consider their originality to be of great value. But I believe we understand nothing, nothing at all, no matter how much we read and study. I believe a confrontation with what's out there will always get you closer to the truth. What's important to me is what's out there, not what I have to say about it. The key is making things available. The art just mediates between people and everything else."

While she was still a student at Bennington, Johanson wrote a term paper in which she explored the consequences of disestablishing the authority of the art object, and working instead with what is given. She claimed, "The world itself would be designed as a work of art."[3] Today she writes of her own work, "Photographs may focus on the object, but the real content of the landscape is everything nature has to offer.... [M]y role as a designer is simply to entice people into landscapes that have their own integrity and their own agenda."[4]

Building *Cyrus Field*, Johanson developed a technique that would allow her to create very large-scale structures without harming the environment. She drew the configurations on graph paper, and then went into the woods. After repeated surveys to accommodate large trees, she set up a grid with stakes and strings. Using garden lime, she transferred the drawing from graph paper to the ground. She says: "This technique has very much to do with not wiping out the natural world, with not bulldozing the site. Of course, if you come in and knock everything down, build your great creation, and plant a few things in place of the complex system you just eradicated, I guess it is easier." Johanson imagines that her method of working has some kinship with how Native Americans laid out large structures like the Serpent Mound in Ohio. Drawing on the land, she sees and responds to the plants and animals around her, changing the drawing to fit the world. She says, "If you see there is a root or a little nest, it's very easy to go around it. You just jog the drawing a little. This is very much the way artists work in their sketchbooks, but you are sketching on the land itself – before building your monumental construction. It's a very low-key way of taking an arbitrary design and placing it on the land in a way that relates to what's already there."

Johanson continues: "If you were to posit a line of cement blocks in a gallery, it would be a pretty dumb thing. But when you put that same line in a forest it suddenly becomes a living thing – interacting with its surroundings, reflecting microhabitats, and moving over the terrain in all kinds of wonderful and unpredictable ways." People respond strongly to *Cyrus Field*. Johanson remembers that when she first built it, most people loved the sculpture, or at least the experience it allowed. As word of *Cyrus Field* spread among Johanson's friends in the New York art world, Bob Morris came up to see it, as did Ellsworth Kelly, Kenneth Noland, Helen Frankenthaler and Robert Motherwell. Sculptor Tony Smith walked through *Cyrus Field* in silence. "I think he was frankly stunned," Johanson says. Photographer Hans Namuth heard about the project and wanted to photograph it. Johanson left him alone in the forest for two hours. When she returned, he was lost and terrified. "I think he was afraid of being eaten," Johanson laughs. Eleanor Munro, visiting to research her book *Originals – American Women Artists* (1979) found the experience of *Cyrus Field* "sheer magic."

When Johanson first received the *House and Garden* commission in 1969, she studied historical gardens: French and Italian formal gardens; romantic English landscapes; Persian, Chinese and Japanese garden traditions. "All landscape compositions seemed to be filled with petty conceits, and I found I really didn't like gardens very much," she remembers. Johanson rejected the notion of designing a landscape with specific views, plantings and pathways that had to be continually maintained. She began thinking about what gardens could be, if they were reconceived as spaces for dialogue between culture and nature. Drawing on her experience with large-scale outdoor painting and sculpture, Johanson realized that if she used line as a compositional basis, nature could be incorporated whole.

In her first proposals for *House and Garden*, she began to develop this idea. In *Exploring the Hills – Bird*, Johanson proposes multi-colored lines that follow the natural terrain over several miles. The art is designed to move people over mountains and through valleys, where the image disappears, and "small details of life predominate" as visitors walk through the "garden." From a bird's-eye-view, on a mountaintop overlook, the overall design reappears, and "art and nature merge and flatten into a homogeneous landscape." In another drawing, *Trail of the Spider Woman: Interstate Natural Highway System*, Johanson expands the idea of a "Line Garden" even further, imaging a continental web of nature corridors traveling over and under two national highway systems, reconnecting disrupted ecosystems and preserving wild landscapes. Johanson comments that Spider Woman in Hopi mythology is the creator of all forms of life. "There are overtones of sculpture in her method; she molds each new being out of earth mixed with her own saliva." With these remarkable designs and many others, Johanson proposes the line as "a strategy for creating non-intrusive, interwoven structures that could be as large as you wished, yet wouldn't be imposing." In the text written to accompany her *House and Garden* proposals in 1969, Johanson notes, "By immersing the person in the real world and by developing an interwoven art of multiple concerns, rather than the monolithic goals of a single designer, the ideal of 'classical perfection' is replaced by the ideal of cooperation and flux. The "Line Garden" becomes a garden of details, linkages, and transitions."[5]

One of the 1969 "Line Gardens" proposes a plan for connecting all the rivers in the United States. Johanson says, "The key concern in my work is bringing human beings, art and nature together. The large vision of *House and Garden* was that you put the world back together again." Whether she is imagining wildlife corridors linking every watershed on the continent, or designing a pedestrian overpass for a single park,

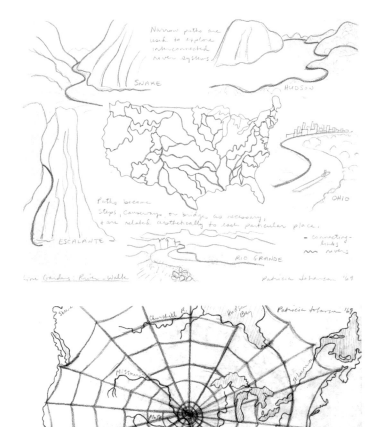

Top: *Line Gardens – River Walk*, 8½" x 11", pencil and colored pencil, 1969

Bottom: *Trail of the Spider Woman: Interstate Natural Highway System*, 8½" x 11", pencil and colored pencil, 1969

Johanson works to create connections. She notes that wild nature needs connected ecosystems to survive. In a 1974 catalogue she writes, "...the artist, as traditional creator of order and poetry out of mundane materials, is perhaps ideally suited to produce a synthesis (or symbiosis) on a larger scale. What is needed is a more reasonable, practical, non-destructive approach to both nature and the man-made environment. Connecting links will go farther toward 'harmony' than more ideal designs. By applying the principles of art broadly and in common-sense ways we will not only add a unifying force to the world – we will also add a purpose and a meaning to our art."

The notion of creating and restoring connections is one Johanson used extensively in her 1999 project in Brockton, Massachusetts. Her plan for this damaged and derelict city involved connecting brooks and rivers to restore watersheds, and connecting neighborhoods that are ethnically and economically divided. Environmental corridors created from existing streets and abandoned lands could bring renewal for people and wildlife. In most urban environments nature is relegated to a decorative amenity. Johanson's plan allows nature to be functional and productive in linear tracts interwoven with urban life.

In 1998 the Massachusetts Cultural Council approached Johanson as they launched a new Cultural Economic Development Program exploring how artists could stimulate the economy. Johanson arrived in Brockton to find a bleak Rust Belt town, vacated by industry when shoe-manufacturing jobs moved to the third world in the 1970s. Drug traffickers occupied abandoned buildings. The City Council had initiated a plan for "urban renewal" that involved knocking down vacant buildings and reducing whole blocks of the city to rubble. Johanson remembers: "I was trying to figure out what an artist could do in a situation like this, and I was really beginning to lose hope." Then while exploring the city she came upon an abandoned house that was the family home of champion heavyweight boxer Rocky Marciano.[6] She listened as "Brockton pride emerged" when people described Marciano's life and achievements. Johanson realized that she had found a key to developing the project. "I saw for the first time that here was something in Brockton that was really unique and special, that people could be proud of."

The Rocky Marciano Trail: Green Streets, Forest and Wildlife Corridors and Stream Restorations Linked to Rocky Marciano's Running Route, 41" x 38", ink, acrylic and colored pencil on printed plan, 1999

The Rocky Marciano Trail, Brockton, Massachusetts, 1997-99

From the beginning, the major goal of my master plan for Brockton has been to unify the landscape visually and functionally, such that disparate neighborhoods and districts are connected, and ecological functioning is restored. In searching for a metaphor that might resonate with Brockton's population, I discovered the boarded-up and deteriorating home of Rocky Marciano, America's only undefeated Heavyweight Boxing Champion, who rose to the top of his profession against all odds. Because he was so poor, Rocky's early training consisted primarily of running through the streets of the city. These seven-mile runs – past mansions, golf courses, woods, fields and streams, around the lakes of a formal park, through the central business district and all the ethnic enclaves – become the thread that unites every neighborhood of the city with nature.

...*The Marciano Trail* consists of three major public sites – *Battery Wagner* and the *Lemuel A. Ashport Swamp Garden*, *Father Thomas McNulty Park*, and the *Rocky Marciano House*. Each site links tourism, community benefit, and infrastructure with ecological restoration. These magnet sites are then connected to each other by means of *Green Streets* –

forest corridors – that in turn are linked to the city's network of small brooks and larger open-spaces: agricultural land, golf courses, parks, wetlands, conservation holdings, and remnant forest on the periphery of the city. Such a plan reinstates the continuity of natural systems throughout the urban fabric.

The *Green Streets* – forest corridors – would be developed as self-maintaining, self-perpetuating systems that encourage native species and connect to the regional landscape. *Green Streets* would help give the city a more coherent visual structure, while clearly separating major traffic arteries from alternative transportation and recreational routes. They would also provide food, habitat, and safe passage for wildlife through the human landscape.

The second major unifying system is the natural path of small wetlands and brooks—now largely paved over, fenced off, channelized, and used as a dumping ground. By reconnecting these waterways physically and visually, restoring their banks and floodplains, and creating a continuous public landscape, fear will be replaced by activities, and the elegance of nature can reemerge as a model for intelligent design.

– Patricia Johanson, 1999

Top: Johanson's plan for Brockton on front page of the *Boston Herald*, May 28, 1998 (reprinted with the permission of the *Boston Herald*)

Bottom: *Intersection of Forest and Traffic Networks*, 8½" x 11", ink and pencil, 1999

The Rocky Marciano Trail, Brockton, Massachusetts, 1997-99 (continued)

Battery Wagner

The site for Brockton's Battery Wagner has flooded for as long as anyone can remember, and despite repeated attempts at engineering, no solution has ever been found. Battery Wagner's structures are therefore designed to reveal the poetry of rising and falling water, rather than the property-damaging floods that occur routinely at this site.

Battery Wagner: Site Plan

Battery Wagner is a magnet river site that combines environmental art, nature, and public space with flood control. It is also a memorial to Lemuel Ashport, Sergeant

William Carney (the first African-American awarded the Congressional Medal of Honor), Frederick Douglass' sons, Lewis and Charles, and other members of the Massachusetts 54th Regiment.

The fort itself is a small-scale replica, constructed as a sculptural earthwork. Because it is a park and playground, the terrible events [of the Civil War battle fought here in 1863] have been transformed into structures that can support the local community while remembering

and honoring the struggle. The moat has become a children's wading pool, with a graded connection to Salisbury Brook for wet-weather overflows.

– Patricia Johanson, 1999

Left: Flooded site of *Battery Wagner*, Brockton, Massachusetts

Right: *Sculpted Flood Plain*, 8½" x 11", pencil and colored pencil, 1969

Facing page: *Battery Wagner/Lemuel A. Ashport Playground*, 30" x 36", acrylic, pastel and ink, 1999

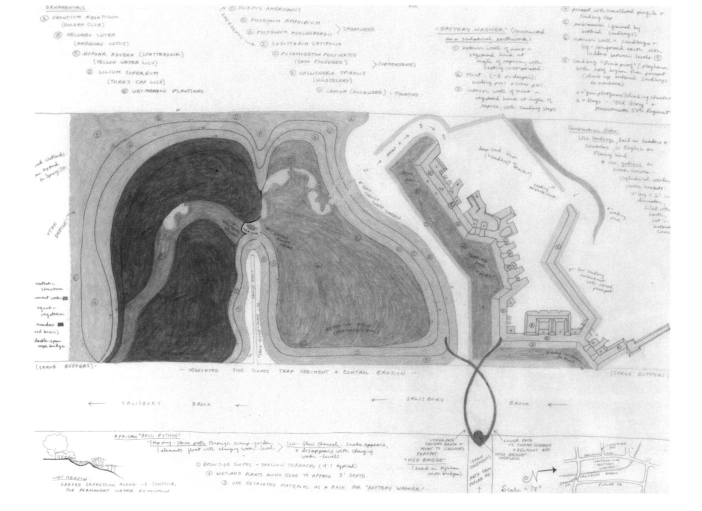

The Rocky Marciano Trail, Brockton, Massachusetts, 1997-99 (continued)

An older city like Brockton, with its abandoned factories, vacant lots, and mixture of urban and suburban patterns that no longer function very well, offers the perfect opportunity to reconsider what form a modern city should take.

It would be much more sensible, aesthetically pleasing, and beneficial to let natural processes determine urban form, so neighborhoods would exist within a matrix of reconnected, self-sustaining, and regenerative nature. Thus, the landscape of Brockton could ameliorate flooding, collect and store drinking water, filter out pollutants, and restore biological richness, while at the same time provide opportunities for recreation and education.

When Rocky Marciano ran through the streets in the late 1940s in his quest to develop strength and stamina, he was presaging the current demand for recreational trails and alternative transportation. We have learned, from an ecological standpoint, that fragmentation destroys the ability of natural systems to function properly (usually at great cost and inconvenience) and kills the life within.

I am committed to gradually restoring functioning biological corridors– urban river and forest– throughout the city. These corridors need to be developed as self-maintaining, self-perpetuating systems that encourage native species, and connect to the larger region. By incorporating the power and intelligence of natural systems into its urban planning strategy, this queen of the industrial age could transform itself into a Mecca of art and culture, nature and livability– as well as a new model for sustainable cities.

– Patricia Johanson, 1998

Father Thomas McNulty Park is at the heart of a downtown revival effort. It combines winter ice-skating and summer water playgrounds with sheep and tourist facilities, housed in traditional Irish structures. The park serves as an entry point to Salisbury Brook's more ecological restored riparian corridor and wildlife habitat, which run through its center.

– Patricia Johanson, 1999

Facing page: *Father McNulty Park*, magnet site along *The Rocky Marciano Trail*, 58½" x 44½", ink and charcoal, 1999

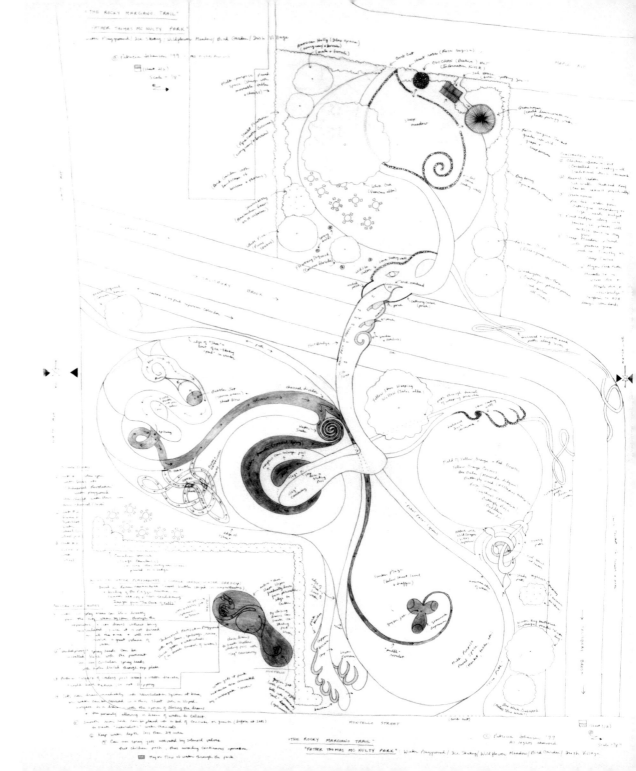

"THE ROCKY MARCIANO TRAIL"

"FATHER THOMAS MC NULTY PARK"

Water Playground / Ice Skating / Wildflower Meadow / Bird Garden / Dutch Village

Marciano's early training runs through ethnically divided neighborhoods and across a variety of landscapes became a unifying image through which Johanson could conceive her project. She proposed *The Rocky Marciano Trail* as a biological corridor connecting disparate neighborhoods and disrupted ecosystems. *Green Streets* could be formed along existing thoroughfares by removing roadbeds, curbs and sidewalks and re-establishing understory plantings and native trees – while still providing vehicle access to residents with narrow, single-lane roads. Tax incentives could encourage private landowners to establish linked naturescapes on private properties. Johanson also conceived of "magnet sites" within *The Rocky Marciano Trail*. *Battery Wagner* and the *Lemuel A. Ashport Swamp Garden*, *Father Thomas McNulty Park*, and *The Rocky Marciano House* were designed to induce tourism, provide infrastructure and layer multiple community benefits. A second major unifying system, reconnecting waterways, involved daylighting brooks and restoring wetlands that had been paved over, fenced off, channelized and used as a dumping ground.

In 1999, writing on "The City as an Ecological Art Form: *The Rocky Marciano Trail*" for the French Ministry of Planning Journal *Les Annales de la Recherche Urbaine*, Johanson says: "Even within cities there is no reason why nature should be relegated to a decorative amenity when its desire is to be functional and productive. Brockton's preponderance of turf is already a strain on the Park Department's budget and staff, and insupportable due to the water shortage, whereas native plants that have co-evolved with the local landscape can prosper. Urban runoff laden with oil, grease, pesticides and organic wastes continue to degrade Brockton's water supply and wetlands, yet green plants and microorganisms could easily remove these harmful substances. Living vegetative filters can double as wildlife habitat, recreation areas, and earth

South Ninth Street Corridor: Railroad, Agriculture, Settler and *Pawnee* medians, 2001

82

sculpture, while at the same time soaking up rainwater and storing it underground for reuse." Though her plans for *The Rocky Marciano Trail* were ultimately rejected by Brockton, Johanson sees the work as a model project for cities.

In 1969, Johanson predicted her Brockton project with an essay on "Gardens for Highways," part of the work developed for *House and Garden* magazine. She wrote: "Perhaps the greatest need, as well as the greatest opportunities, would exist along roads that move through 'ugly,' underprivileged, or industrial areas." In this radical essay, the young artist proposed highways as "potentially the largest gardens in the world." One drawing, *Regional Highway Garden: Muskrats*, suggests that an existing highway, moving through marshland, could be treated aesthetically to suggest a muskrat's tail-mark, while marshy ponds in the shape of muskrat footprints would house real muskrats living in native ecosystems. With such projects developed on the public land now consisting of traffic arteries and drainage systems, "...highways might recapture some sense of character and place, instead of the antiseptic monotony that stretches from coast to coast," becoming "unifying elements that [link] communities, instead of dividing them." Johanson concludes her essay with the startling concept that "Highway Gardens invite people to explore the world by providing interwoven systems – places within places – and by organizing and presenting the world as a work of art."

More than thirty years later, Johanson was invited to design a "Highway Garden" in Salina, Kansas on a percent-for-art commission. Her designs for a series of nondescript highway drainage medians 60-feet-wide by 600-feet-long imply a new vision for the country's roads. With historical information, habitat components and public access, the

Above left: South Ninth Street with park site/drainage medians along right.

Right: *South Ninth Street Corridor, Petroglyph/Coronado Heights* median, Salina, Kansas, 2001

Facing page far right: Concrete channel within drainage median

South Ninth Street Corridor, The History of Salina, Salina, Kansas, 2001

The History of Salina, sited in functional drainage medians between South Ninth Street (US 81) and the frontage roads, presents a series of miniature landscapes visualizing this place during various historical periods. The goal is to enhance the highway by incorporating art, landscaping, and a public trail within a design unique to the local area....

The corridor begins with fossil images from past geological eras, including a giant dragonfly, a fossil fern from the Western Inland Sea, and a pteranodon, whose wingspan approximated a small airplane. Other sculptural landscapes relate to Coronado's journey, native petroglyphs, a Pawnee Earth Lodge, sod dwelling, "bleeding Kansas," agriculture and the railroad. A continuous trail, based on the meandering Smoky Hill River, links the sculptural features. A larger route through the entire city reveals many of the actual places that are referenced within the park-like *South Ninth Street Corridor*.

Features along the Corridor:

...Two undulating buffalo grass terraces form the image of a Buckeye Butterfly, an insect that will be attracted to this site by specific plantings. The "eyespot" patterns of the butterfly– a free-form hill and two dome-shaped mounds – are translated into Pawnee Earth Lodges, which function as seating and overlooks.

The largest Pawnee Earth Lodge, twenty-two feet in diameter with a six-foot high

exterior roof, has a tunnel-like entrance dug down into the ground. The lodge opens up into a twelve-foot high domed interior with a continuous perimeter bench, and sky visible through the spacious "smoke hole" above. Astronomy governed every aspect of Pawnee life and the palpable connection between earth and sky and the movements of nature are made visible as constellations of stars, such as "The Circle of Chiefs," are framed and pulled down into the lodge.

Earth lodges were traditionally used by the Pawnee as outdoor seating and vantage points, and the grassy roof will reveal the patterns of both the Buckeye Butterfly and the Bull Snake, whose green tail moves across the intersection onto gently rolling topography with tallgrass prairie.

Elongated, undulating berms frame the path as the buffalo grass "snake" meanders toward the higher "hills" in the distance. As one enters the "valley," the path adds the reddish-brown markings of the Bull Snake, like a musical beat. The berms are now sloping gently upward on both sides of the path, making it possible to walk along the crest of the "hills," or sit on top and watch the action below.

At the highest point, a "chimney" seat offers a clue to this miniaturization of the Smoky Valley, as the body of the snake rolls over the roof of a Sod House below. Early settlers often dug their homes into the sides of hills, and snakes would frequently get into the roof and fall down on unsuspecting inhabitants. The huge size of the buffalo grass snake, compared to the tiny hand-cut sod bricks that comprise the walls of the house, dramatically demonstrates how greatly the balance was tipped in favor of nature in those days. . . .

86

Nestled within the shadow of the bull snake lies a red "rosebud" that echoes the form of the snake's head and continues across the intersection as a slender green "stem." At either end of the drainage median, topographical undulating berms with small paths and seating areas are patterned after patchwork quilt flowers and planted with alfalfa (culture and agriculture).

Wild alfalfa, native to the prairie, is now a cultivated crop. Its purple flowers attract many butterflies, including Yellow Sulphurs, and the dense plantings are intensely green when not in bloom. In winter the parterre shapes, based on a patchwork rose and lily, come to the fore.

....Walking through the drainage ditch, a green "stem path" weaves up and down the slopes between tall rows of corn – the first crop planted in the sod. This intimate personal experience of agriculture will be enhanced by seasonal changes in growth, texture, and color—from green, to golden, to brown. Standing crops will remain through the winter as wildlife food and habitat, ensuring the sounds and activities of many creatures.

Across the intersection the "railroad track" path splits into a route that parallels South Ninth Street and a "spur" that curves around the end of the median and connects with a concrete flume and grassy swale that descends into the drainage ditch. The "sunflower walk" places pedestrians inside a field of sunflowers, with the plants rising on both sides of the gently sloping ditch. The shape of fields and path echo a traditional quilting pattern—the "cable"—and as the vista narrows and widens it offers intimate and more distant views of the sunflower's powerful stalks and massive "heads," impressive in any season.

The blue "Smoky Hill River" path crosses the "sunflower walk," connecting to both the frontage road and South Ninth Street, or pedestrians can continue walking down into a massive concrete drainage channel that conveys water under the roadways. Step/seating provides a natural gathering place, as well as an exit from the drainage infrastructure. With appropriate curb cuts and slopes, this step/seating can also become a "water cascade" generated by rainstorms. The entire median is edged in black– the "soil" that attracted settlers, whose land-grant purchases paid for the railroad. A shady bench with arched "railroad tunnel" arbor frames the drainage channel. Both sunflowers (left as a standing crop) and grape arbor plantings will attract birds as well as tourists.

– Patricia Johanson, 2001, unpublished
   manuscript titled "South Ninth Street
   Corridor, The History of Salina"

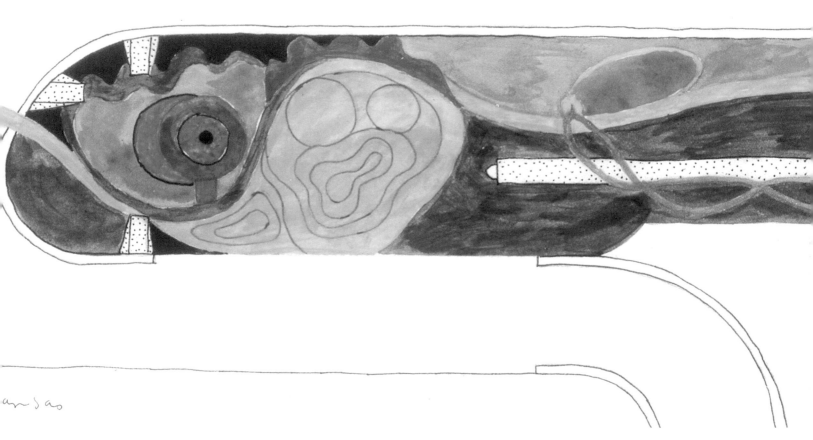

Facing page: *South Ninth Street Corridor,*
Fossil Fern median, 2001
Above: *South Ninth Street Corridor*, (detail),
Pawnee Earth Lodge within Buckeye
Butterfly, 2001

project develops a complex narrative line that unfolds for park users and passing motorists.

"I was attracted to Salina because the landscape is so typical. It's basically a commercial strip," Johanson says. She explains: "When I take on a project, I start by trying to educate people – so they can expand their vision. Instead of just decorating something with a piece of sculpture, I want them to understand how much more they could accomplish just by shifting their vision a little."

Johanson proposes a sculptural walking path, bike trail, works of art and landscaping within the drainage medians and dangerous intersections along Highway 81, designed so that people and animals can use this space as part of a continuous trail through the city. Sequential landscapes and built structures tell the story of Salina during various epochs, while also providing park features including seating, shelter, fountains and overlooks. Johanson reflects, "Because it was a highway, because it was long and linear, I knew I was going to have to do something that would develop in physical time and space." She conceived the project using a narrative line based on the area's natural and cultural history. Again in Salina, Johanson's design links art with infrastructure, weaving together social functions and natural systems.

NOTES:

1 Johanson, 1974.

2 Johanson, 2003, p. 102.

3 Johanson, c. 1960, "Some Italian Renaissance Cities," term paper written for a class taught by Tony Smith.

4 Johanson, 2003, p. 75.

5 Johanson, 1969, "Gardens by the mile... the line garden."

6 This project is described in detail in C. Rotella, 2002, *Good With Their Hands*, Berkeley: University of California Press.

Facing page: *Roads Painted Different Colors*, 8¼" x 11½", colored pencil on book illustration, 1966

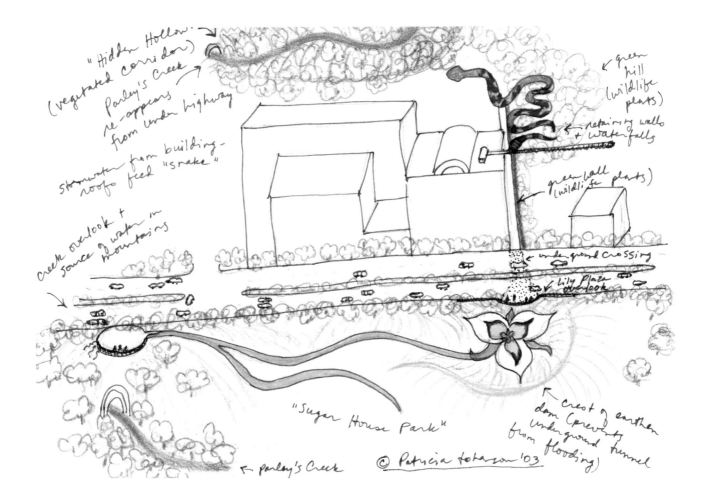

"Hidden Hollow"
(vegetated corridor)
Parley's Creek
re-appears
from under highway

Stormwater from building-
roofs feed "snake"

green
hill
(wildlife
plants)

retaining walls
+ waterfalls

green wall
(wildlife plants)

Creek overlook +
source ? water in
source ? mountains

underground crossing

lily plaza
overlook

"Sugar House Park"

crest of earthen
dam (prevents
underground tunnel
from flooding)

← Parley's Creek   © Patricia Johanson '03

FUNCTIONAL LANDSCAPES

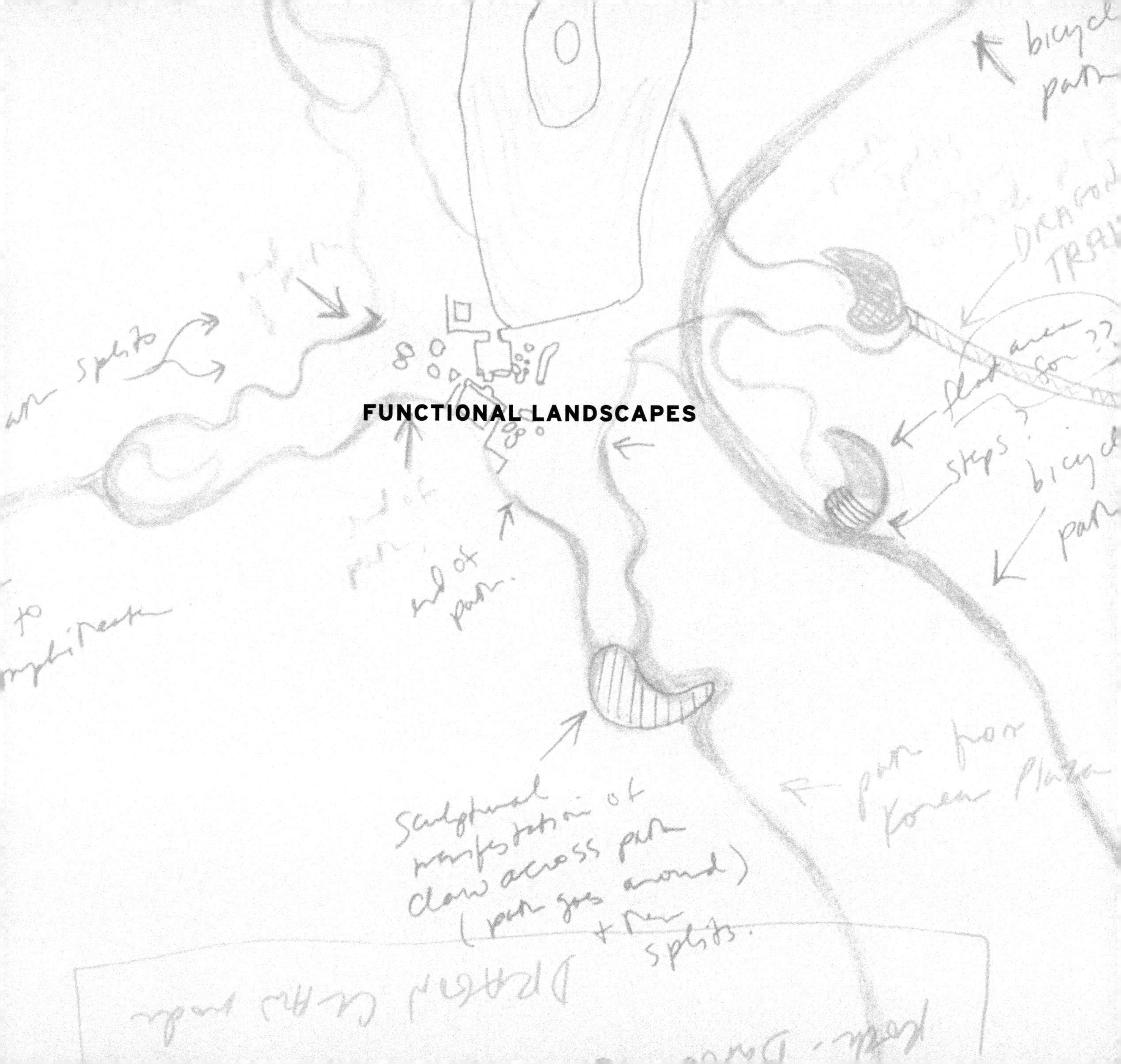

bicycle path

DRAGON TRAIL

flat area for??

steps?

bicycle path

win splits

to amphitheater

end of path.

end of path.

Sculptural manifestation of claw across park (park goes around) + now splits.

← path from Korean Plaza

"Vernal Pools" (Catagramma minora) - Park / Amphibian Breeding Grounds / Edible Landscaping   © Patricia Johanson '92

(Bridge Crossing Vernal Pools)

FUNCTIONAL LANDSCAPES

JOHANSON WAS IN HER TWENTIES WHEN SHE FIRST IMAGINED INTEGRATING ART, ecology and infrastructure. A drawing from 1966 describes *Roads Painted Different Colors*. While doing research for the *House and Garden* commission in 1969, Johanson's interest was engaged by functional landscapes. She wrote: "The art of survival – systems that provide pure drinking water, food, and flood control – has produced some of the most beautiful gardens in the world."[1] Inspired by "Roman aqueducts, Inca irrigation and terracing ... and the vast networks of jetties, dams and levees along our major rivers," Johanson developed designs for gardens made from flood plains, reservoirs and drainage systems. She realized that her training as an artist, with everything she knew about color, shape, form, and the relationship between spectator and object, could be used to address practical problems and built structures in the real world. She envisioned creating functioning garbage gardens, highway gardens and gardens made from the structure of cities.

In 1969, Johanson's *House and Garden* drawing *Municipal Water Gardens: Channels* proposed a public landscape that provides wildlife habitat, processes sewage and welcomes visitors. This early vision of a multi-functioning landscape – both beautiful and useful – informs Johanson's current work on a $130 million facility for the city of

Previous pages, left: *Sugar House Pedestrian Crossing, sketch*, Salt Lake City, Utah, 7⅛" x 10⅝", ink and colored pencil, 2003

Right: *Dragon Claw Node, Ulsan Park*, Korea, 17¼" x 15½", colored pencil and ink, 1996

Facing page: *Vernal Pools (Catagramma mionina): Park/Amphibian Breeding Grounds/Edible Landscaping*, 42" x 44", ink, charcoal and gouache, 1992

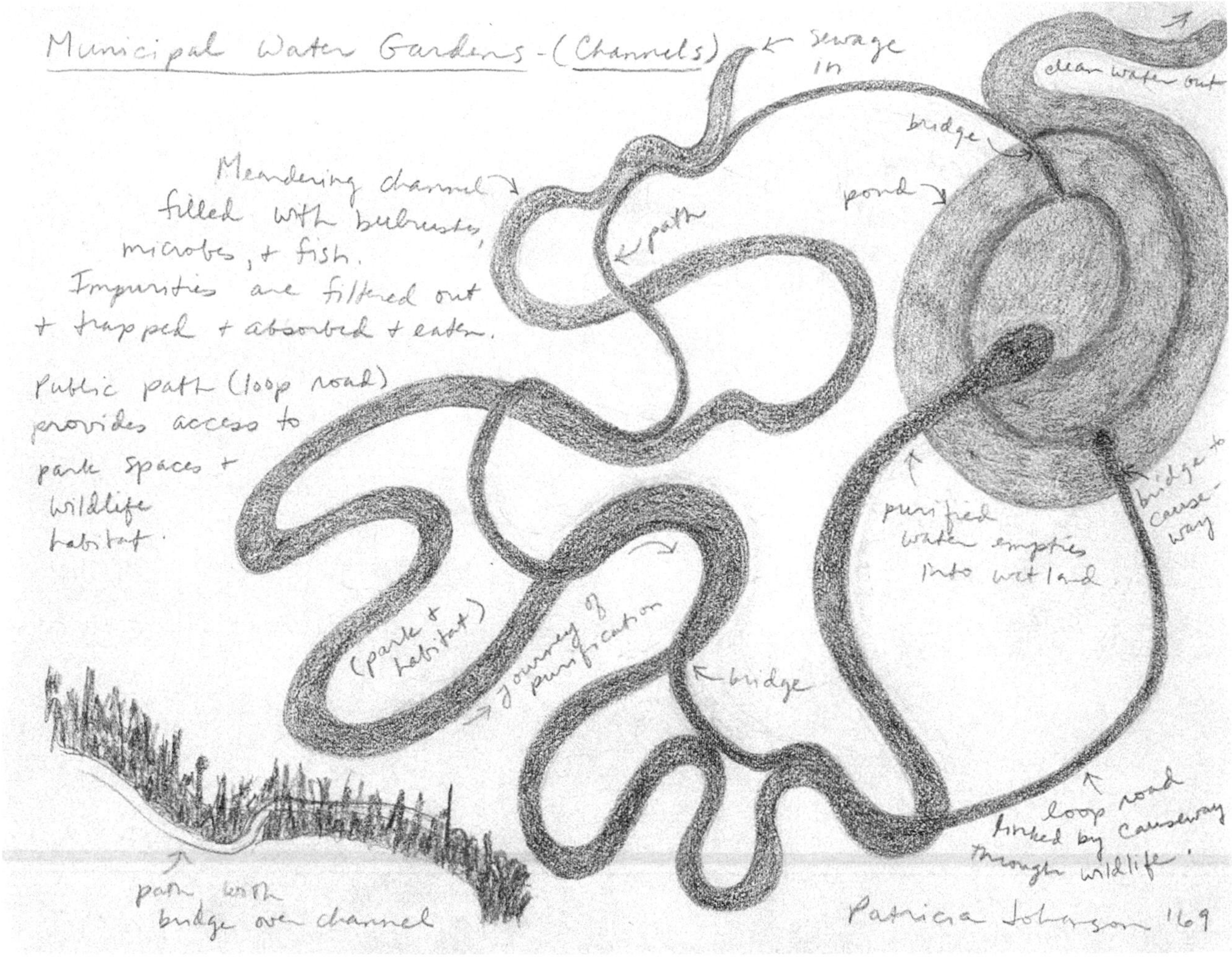

94

Municipal Water Gardens - (Channels)

← sewage in

clean water out

Meandering channel → filled with bulrushes, microbes, + fish.
Impurities are filtered out + trapped + absorbed + eaten.

Public path (loop road) provides access to park spaces + wildlife habitat.

← path

pond →

bridge

(park + habitat)

→ Journey of purification

purified water empties into wetland.

bridge to causeway

← bridge

loop road linked by causeway through wildlife.

path with bridge over channel

Patricia Johanson '69

Petaluma, California. The Petaluma project includes treatment wetlands and polishing ponds – landscapes that process sewage – within a 272-acre park that is a mosaic of restored ecosystems.

The little Salt Marsh Harvest Mouse, an endangered species, is a unifying image for this enormous project. More than three miles of public trails and interpretive sites reveal the intricacies of wastewater treatment, the tidal cycle, the ever-changing patterns of land and water and the complex relationships between ecosystems. The natural zonation of the landscape moves from tidal mudflats and marshes along the river to agricultural fields and upland habitats along the highway and business park. Johanson says: "Images give people a way to approach the projects. This is a little mouse that will live on the site in pickleweed surrounding the southernmost polishing pond, which is part of the sewage treatment train. The mouse's eyes become islands where waterbirds such as rails and avocets can rest and nest."

In 2002, Johanson was hired by the city of Petaluma as a member of the Carollo Engineers design team to create a new sewer facility. A wetlands park was not part of the initial project. Johanson describes her creative process: "I walked along a breached levee one day and saw how beautiful it was with the tide rushing in. Another day, I witnessed birds feeding on the mudflats when the tide was out. I could see the power and importance of this site, and I felt it just had to become part of the project." She realized that if the city were to acquire this adjoining parcel of vacant land, it would be an appropriate location for polishing wetlands. In addition, it would allow a tidal wetlands park to be linked to the sewage treatment project. "I made a small drawing – as I often do, just as a visioning process – to show people what was possible." One night at a city council meeting, Johanson presented her concept. She talked about the tidal wetlands wedged between Sonoma Mountain and Olompali – once the largest Native-American settlement in California. She described the ecological value of building fresh-water polishing ponds adjacent to brackish wetlands, creating habitat for many different species of animals and birds. She also described the park as an economic development project that would bring people to Petaluma, supporting local hotels

Municipal Water Gardens: Channels, 8½" x 11", pencil and colored pencil, 1969

Petaluma Wetlands Park and Water Recycling Facility, Petaluma, California, 2001-05

I am currently working with Carollo Engineers on a new $130 million dollar water recycling facility for the city of Petaluma, California. The project includes oxidation ponds, sewage treatment wetlands and polishing ponds for the removal of heavy metals, as well as a new 272-acre tidal marsh and mudflat: Petaluma Wetlands Park. As a designer I have always been interested in enmeshing human needs within the larger patterns and purposes of nature. In Petaluma, art and infrastructure, ecological nature and the public landscape, are unified within the image of one of the area's smallest inhabitants – the "Salt Marsh Harvest Mouse." More than three miles of public trails and

interpretive sites trace the patterns of the creature, while revealing the intricacies of wastewater treatment, the tidal cycle, ever-changing patterns of land and water, and the complex relationships between microhabitats and ecosystems.

At the heart of the Wetlands Park, four elevated bermed ponds totaling 30 acres form the mouse's image. Habitat islands in each sewage treatment cell offer protected nesting and refuge for birds, while also directing the flow of water in the basins. The aesthetics of wastewater treatment is further defined by broad "green" bands of vegetation, alternating with "blue" bands of deeper open water (habitat for predatory fish). Within the green zones suspended solids are being consumed by microscopic aquatic animals and insects that live on plants, while these same plants pump oxygen into

their submerged stems, roots, and tubers, supplying the microbial decomposers.

Vegetation and substrate varies on islands within each of the polishing ponds, as do shoreline conditions, in order to attract a wide range of different species. The Mouse Pond (Cell D of the polishing wetlands) [see page ii] provides barren islands for water bird nesting (for species such as the Black-Necked Stilt, American Avocet, and Forster's Tern); beaches for foraging; and wildlife food and habitat plantings. A grape-arbor and pavilion in one of the mouse's "ears" conceals three separate blinds focusing on the littoral zone, a nesting island and Ellis Creek. Amphitheater seating in the other "ear" forms a gathering space for small groups, while the mouse's "nose" provides an

Continued on page 99

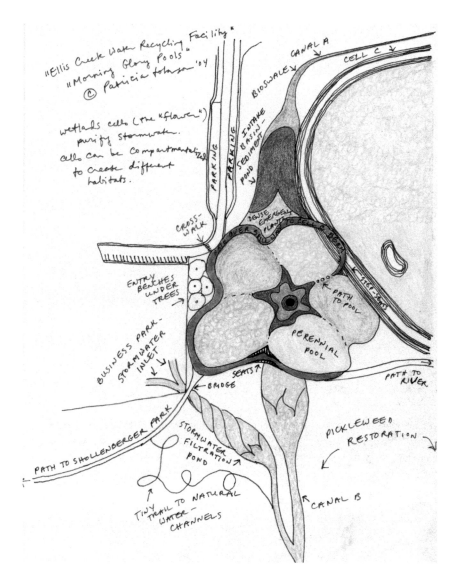

Facing page, top left: *Ellis Creek Water Recycling Facility*, Petaluma, California: aerial photo shows entire site, with Petaluma River (bottom), tidal wetlands (lower left) with site for polishing ponds above, and ten oxidation ponds (right) (photo: Scott Hess)

Top right: *Petaluma Wetlands Park* at low tide with Olompali, an historic Miwok city (now Mount Burdell) in background (photo: Scott Hess)

This page: *Ellis Creek Water Recycling Facility: Morning Glory Pools*, 11" x 8⅝", ink, pastel and colored pencil, 2004

97

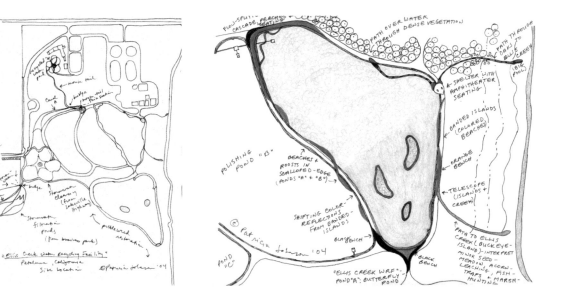

98

Left: *Ellis Creek Water Recycling Facility, Petaluma California: Site Location,* 10⅞" x 9⅛", ink and pencil, 2004

Right: *Ellis Creek Water Recycling Facility, Petaluma, California: Pond A: Butterfly Pond,* 8¾" x 11", acrylic, ink and colored pencil, 2004

Facing page: *Ellis Creek Water Recycling Facility: Mouse Tail Thin Section,* 22" x 8¾", ink, pastel and colored pencil, 2004

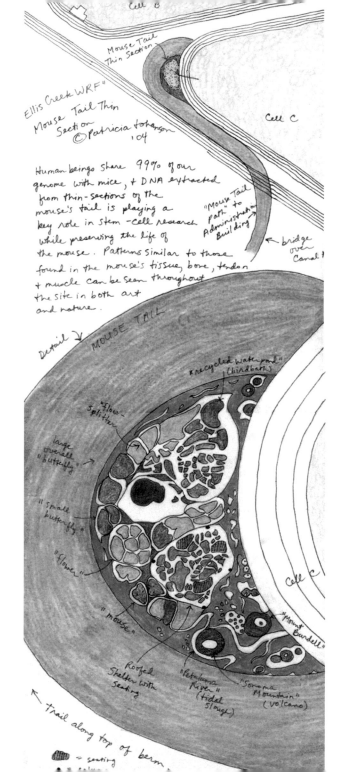

Continued from page 96

overlook for interpreting the densely vegetated treatment wetlands, pump-station and marshy expanse leading to the Petaluma River. . . .

Petaluma Wetlands Park unifies massive man-made landscapes organized for food production, sewage processing, and water purification, with many layers of public and ecological benefit – from wildlife habitat restorations and school educational programs to recreation, tourism and art. Perhaps most importantly, it serves as a model for converting sewage to drinkable water. One of my missions as a designer is to create inclusive life-supporting landscapes that broaden human understanding. Artists have always changed the way we see. Now we need to change the way we act. The new wholeness and harmony lies not in design perfection but in our ability to bring competing populations, interests and points of view together harmoniously in the real world. Ultimately my projects seek design solutions that are as creative, functional and biologically productive as nature itself.

– Patricia Johanson, 2004, unpublished manuscript titled "Water Recycling Facility and Petaluma Wetlands Park, Petaluma, California: Design Narrative"

and restaurants. "People caught the vision. A group of local citizens formed the Petaluma Wetlands Park Alliance, and the project became a reality," she says.

Like the Petaluma project, Johanson's design for a landfill closure in Seoul, Korea emerges from drawings she made more than 35 years ago. In 1969, Johanson made a design for "Garbage Gardens creat[ing] sculptural topography out of organic waste." In another drawing, *Turtle Mound*, she imagined a landfill designed as garden and sculpture. In 1999, Johanson was part of an international team of experts invited to envision solutions for a 90-meter high dumpsite, which loomed menacingly over the World Cup Soccer Stadium. This enormous mound of household and industrial waste was located along a major highway between Kimpo International Airport and City Hall. Johanson remembers: "We were taken to the site where we were hauled up to the top of the landfill and nearly overcome by methane gas!" Recognizing that no design concept could hide this mountain of garbage, she imagined it as a park devoted to human recreation and wildlife habitat. "I said to them, 'Yes, it is a landfill. But it's also the most magnificent overlook you have in the city. Terrace the slopes, stabilize the landfill and create hiking trails all over this mountain.' "

The unifying image for *Millennium Park* is a haetae guardian figure. During the Choson Dynasty, it was common to install haetae figures near bridges or buildings, where these mythical animals were thought to defend against fire, drought and invading enemies. Johanson was engaged by these sculptures as she explored the city. She photographed a favorite haetae figure at Kyongbokkung Palace in downtown Seoul, and made a drawing that reconfigured the haetae as public trails that stabilized the landfill. She says, "Basically what I did was leave the landfill intact, and sculpt it with terracing, creating a monument that everyone would relate to – a great guardian figure that stands between North and South Korea, protecting the city of Seoul." In *Millennium Park*, Johanson envisions the landfill problem as an occasion for multiple benefits.

Daring for art to have a function "[calls] into question the very framework within which we define art," notes Amy Lipton.[2] Johanson describes the place of art in Western tradition as "segregated in culture palaces where it is only available to five percent of people, and where it has very little meaning for our everyday life." She comments: "Artists have tremendous energy and vision that go to waste in the tiny, closely guarded world of art. Right now we don't need any more art that takes up space for no reason. We need art that engages people deeply, and mechanisms for bringing that art into a functional relationship with the social and natural world. It's just impossible to deal with the world in terms of formal relationships at a point when our survival is at stake."

The notion of a utilitarian art has precedents that inspire Johanson. Her sense of art's capacity to transform ordinary life is deeply influenced by the role art plays in traditional cultures. In Petaluma, Johanson found the site had a long history of human culture interwoven with productivity and natural processes. By 1400, Olompali was one of the largest urban trading centers on the West Coast, and its inhabitants, the Coast Miwok, caught salmon and steelhead trout along Ellis Creek with weirs (stakes pounded into the stream bed and interwoven with willow branches and tules) – designed to funnel fish into beautiful hand woven basket traps. Magnificent duck decoys and branching deer headdresses aided in the process of hunting. Johanson notes: "Today we might call these artifacts 'sculpture' or 'site-specific art.' The Miwok, however, did not separate art from daily life, nor did they feel unrelated to natural phenomena or processes. They believed a wide patch of moonlight on the ocean was the pathway to the spirit world, and their narrow beaten trails were sunk into the surrounding landscape, where every grove of trees, rock and resting place had a name. The Coast Miwok lived in a unified world where life and death, seasons and cycles, art and process, were all part of the same design."[3]

Eighteenth and nineteenth century American artists – whom Johanson researched extensively while completing her masters degree in American art history at Hunter College – are part of a largely unexplored utilitarian tradition in American art. In addition to the research involved in completing her degree and a thesis on limner painter Ralph Earl (1751-1801), Johanson worked for publisher Benjamin Blom researching and writing a compendium on American artists of the eighteenth and nineteenth centuries. Johanson describes her attraction to these artists: "Many of these painters were

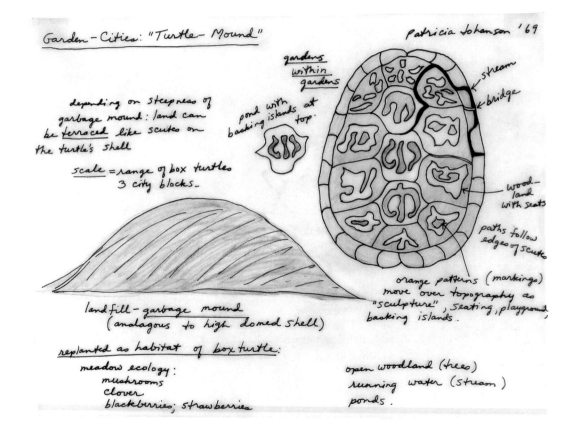

Garden – Cities: "Turtle – Mound"

Patricia Johanson '69

gardens
within
gardens

depending on steepness of
garbage mound: land can
be terraced like scutes on
the turtle's shell

scale = range of box turtles
3 city blocks.

pond with
basking islands at
top.

stream

bridge

wood-
land
with seats

paths follow
edges of scutes

landfill – garbage mound
(analogous to high domed shell)

orange patterns (markings)
move over topography as
"sculpture", seating, playground,
basking islands.

replanted as habitat of box turtle:
meadow ecology:
mushrooms
clover
blackberries; strawberries

open woodland (trees)
running water (stream)
ponds.

MILLENIUM PARK · SEOUL · KOREA · 1999

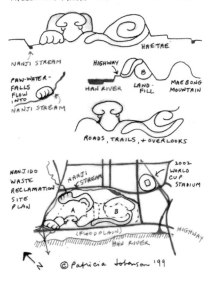

Facing page: *Garden-Cities: Turtle Mound*, 8½" x 11", pencil and ink, 1969

This page, top: *Millenium Park* landfill site, Seoul, Korea

Bottom: *Millenium Park*, Seoul, Korea, 7" x 5", 1999

Millennium Park, Seoul, South Korea, 1999

Nanji Island was originally a small landmass within the Han River known for its flora and fauna. In 1978, it became the main waste dumpsite for the city of Seoul, with no soil coverage and no separation of household and industrial wastes. Vertical filling continued until 1990 when the landfill—now over ninety meters high—was closed.

The reclamation project has recently taken on added urgency because the enormous landfill, with a polluted Nanji Stream at its base, dwarfs the new 2002 World Cup Soccer Stadium where opening ceremonies will be held. Because portions of the site are regularly flooded during the rainy season there is also the danger of polluted leachates seeping into Nanji Stream and flowing into the Han River, which runs through the heart of Seoul. In 1999, the Seoul Development Institute assembled a team of international experts to design a blueprint for the sustainable development of Nanjido, and transform the dumpsite into *Millennium Park*.

During the Choson Dynasty, it was common to install haetae—a mythical animal that warded off evil—near a bridge or building. These carved stone sculptures with their crouching stance, powerful claws, bulging eyes and decorative patterned scales often emerge

unexpectedly from the landscape. In a similar manner, the Nanjido Waste Reclamation Site appears without warning, overshadowing the natural mountains that rise behind it, as well as the Han River and eight-lane highway at its base. Decorative patterning on haetae figures often resembles traditional Korean rice-paddy farming—the same kind of terracing that would be required to stabilize the landfill's side slopes and create smaller microhabitats within the monolithic mass. These terraced levels not only define the animal's image—they also serve as hiking paths, stairways, overlooks and vehicle access roads to the twin summits, which are separated by a broad central valley resulting from the dumping process.

The current goal envisions a park atop the western eminence, while restoring self-sustaining ecological communities to the eastern landmass, serving both the public, as well as native plants and animals within the urban landscape. As Korea's newest guardian of longevity, health, recreation, and even the natural world, the mythical beast continues to ward off evil. *Millennium Park* becomes both a powerful symbol, and a powerful reality of public waste transformed into public wealth.

– Patricia Johanson, 1999, unpublished manuscript

naturalists. They made beautiful drawings of plants and animals, native tribes and their artifacts and the local landscape. They were recording everything in a very scientific, descriptive way – and I've always appreciated that. Their drawings and paintings conveyed information and often had notes on the side, just like my drawings. These artists had social, environmental and educational goals behind what they were representing."

Johanson contrasts this tradition with the self-referential discourse surrounding contemporary art. "Art feeds upon art, so you get an ever-diminishing dialogue," she says. Johanson became frustrated with the limits of this discourse while still a young student at Bennington College. She remembers: "One of the buzzwords was, 'You have to find your own image.' People wanted 'a Noland' or 'a Frankenthaler,' a 'Kelly' or a 'Motherwell.' They wanted art to be recognizable products. Those artists who fit within the commercial gallery scene were very much boxed into their images. It was difficult for them to move beyond that, because their dealers would have been deeply unhappy. These painters got boxed in by their success, and I've never been willing to let that happen. I've always been more interested in exploring ideas."

With the notion of usefulness, Johanson distinguishes her work from other trends in public and environmental art. "There has probably never been a time when more lip service was paid to the idea of 'public art' – with such dismal results," she says. "Until the barriers are broken down between aesthetic, functional and ecological – between what is art, architecture and landscape – it's unlikely that much of the built world will be livable, let alone have the power to move and inspire." Given the present understanding of the role art can play in the public realm, an artist may be hired to decorate a site such as a landfill closure. But with a small shift in thinking, artists could simultaneously create habitat and make the site available to different constituencies. What if, through the creativity of artists, landfills, airports, sewers and highways could become parks, playgrounds, restored ecosystems and recreational facilities? Johanson reflects that with the right kind of planning, such work need not cost any more than capping a landfill, or filling a site with decorative objects intended to ameliorate the "ugliness" of the place.

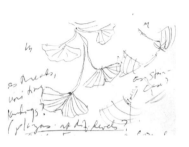

Above: *Ginko Plazas*, sketch, 3¼" x 4", red ink, c. 1974

Right: *Garden with Snapdragon Fountains*, 24" x 36", ink and charcoal, 1974

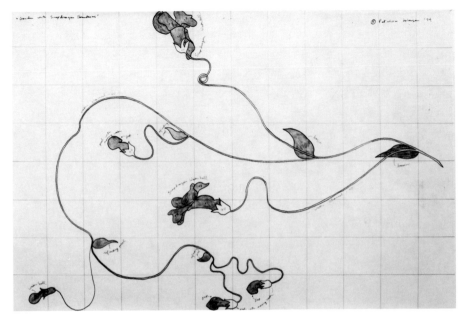

Johanson contrasts the plight of homeless people with the work of artists building sculptures on the subject of homelessness. She says, "Instead of making objects that people admire for their colors, forms and ideal relationships, artists could work with the same aesthetic concerns and simultaneously be building shelter for those who need it."

The role of artists in functional projects may be problematic as well as promising. When artists cooperate with government and industry to build infrastructure or restore industrial sites, do they become complicit in an effort to reassure the public about sinister forces pushing indefensible agendas? Describing his own work in land reclamation, Robert Morris writes that when his project received sponsorship from the U.S. Bureau of Mines, he realized that "art must then stand accused of contributing its energy to forces that are patently, cumulatively destructive."[4] Johanson is undeterred by such considerations. She gauges each project with the simple question: "Is this lead-

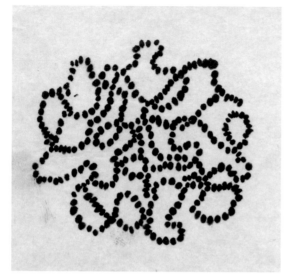

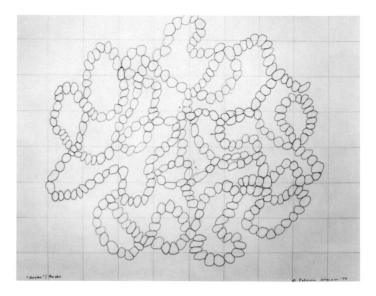

Above left: "Nostoc" sketch translates pattern of the algae chain into "rocks" on a scrap of paper, 4½" x 4¾", ink, c. 1974

Above right: *Nostoc/Rocks*, 24" x 30", ink, 1974

Below right: *Blue-Green Algae (Nostoc)*, scale plan, 4¾" x 3" notebook, red and blue ink, c. 1974

Facing page: *Nostoc II*, 30' x 49'3" x 40'9", stone, 1975. Collection: Storm King Art Center, Mountainville, New York, gift of the Ralph E. Ogden Foundation, Inc. (photo: Jerry L. Thompson)

Nostoc/Rocks

Like all blue-green algae, "Nostoc" is closely related to the bacteria, yet contains chlorophyll. Its unspecialized cells form twisted, coiled filaments embedded in a gelatinous matrix – here interpreted as a chain of rocks, interwoven with the landscape. Varying heights, colors, and facets of the rocks, plus variations in plants, trees, and terrain produce a sculpture of great complexity that changes with every shift of wind, light, and shadow.

– Patricia Johanson, 1978

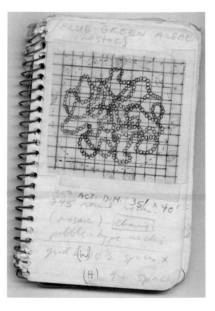

ing toward a more benevolent world?" When she can answer in the affirmative, she applies her creativity whole-heartedly to the issues at hand. She says, "I'd like to expunge my ego as an artist and just do work that is positive and life-supporting."

Johanson's commitment to creating places with multiple purposes is deeply informed by the time she spent drawing and researching plants in the 1970s. Attending to the minutiae of the natural world while creating the *Plant Drawings for Projects* changed her focus from aesthetic to functional goals.

"This series made it possible to free myself from my design training. Just drawing these plants removed me from the whole process of art history and immersed me in the world of nature and function. I began to understand things differently. Instead of asking only 'How does it look?' I began to ask 'What is this plant's strategy?' 'How does it work?'" Through studying botany, biology and ecology, Johanson discovered that "nature doesn't do anything that's frivolous. No matter how bizarre a form looks, it's there for a very specific reason." With the *Plant Drawings for Projects* Johanson began to use the structures of nature as a way of thinking. "In nature everything is purposeful," she says. "Biological strategies are blueprints for survival. Each plant is not only an architectural structure. It's also a reproduction strategy, a how-to-get-water strategy, a how-to-reach-the-sunlight strategy." In the 1970s, Johanson made hundreds of plans and drawings for buildable structures based on the design strategies of the natural world.

Johanson's work suggests a new approach to design and building that uses natural patterns as the basis for all human activity. Celebrated educator and design consultant William McDonough[5] suggests a similar conceptual shift. He notes that growth is not necessarily a destructive goal for countries and industries, if humans could learn to grow like trees. The growth of trees produces oxygen, transpires water, nourishes ecosystems and creates microhabitats. Leaves, seeds, blossoms and bark cast off in the process of growth and decay all become food for other forms of life. Revisioning human capacities by designing through the structures and strategies of nature is a practice Johanson first undertook in her *House and Garden* drawings. On the drawing for one proposal, *Water Gardens: Stormwater Runoff*, she writes, "The design strategy of a plant – stems and leaves – are arranged to counter problem flooding...." The concept of using nature-based design patterns to build structures with multiple benefits appears repeatedly in Johanson's early work. Her careful study of biology and plant physiology while creating the *Plant Drawings for Projects* shaped her vision. When she had the opportunity to physically build a project in Dallas, she witnessed the power of this design strategy to restore living ecosystems. Johanson experienced the excitement and truth of her insight that art could "repair the broken connections – and make a place 'whole' again."

Surviving cancer in the 1980s sharpened Johanson's focus on creating structures with multiple ecological and social benefits. "I started looking at environmental problems – threatened species, depleted soil, toxic landfills, poisoned water – and trying to think about how solutions to these problems could become part of public parks," she says. One of the first projects Johanson undertook after her cancer treatments was a series of simple designs for *Survival Sculptures*. She conceived of sculptural forms dug into the ground beside contaminated rivers, filled with oxygenating plants and microorganisms that would cleanse and filter pollutants. Polluted water, diverted through these sculptures, flows back to the river clear, clean and safe. Johanson describes the forms of the *Survival Sculptures* as inspired by river meanders. "That's why they're so simple and appealing," she says. "The sculptures are based on how water flows, so they resonate with memories of other bodies of water – rivers, streams, creeks, rivulets, falling drops of water, and the way they all come together in a watershed. Then you also see the larger image of the meandering snake, spider or human hand. It's a creature, filled with plants, animals and microorganisms. These are human-made, aesthetic bodies of water that perform important functions and then flow back into natural bodies of water."

The *Survival Sculptures* were originally made as drawings for an exhibit – there was no specific site envisioned for the work. The exhibit led to an invitation to work in Kenya on a project to cleanse the Nairobi River. Using wetland plants and microorganisms as water-purifiers made the sculptures particularly appropriate for Africa, where reliance on sophisticated technologies supplied by industrialized countries can create

"Survival Sculpture"   © Patricia Johanson '90

Above: *Survival Sculpture*, 5¼" x 12", acrylic and ink, 1990

Facing page left: *Nairobi River Park*, site photo showing polluted river, 1995

Right: Sketch for *Survival Sculptures* (detail), pencil, ink and colored pencil, 1990

Page 112: *Survival Sculpture (Water Purification): Snake*, 18" x 18", acrylic and ink, 1990

Page 113: *Survival Sculpture (Water Purification): Hand*, 18" x 18", acrylic and ink, 1990

Survival Sculptures, 1990
Nairobi River Park, Kenya, 1995

I am currently designing a park in Nairobi, Kenya, where many people still believe deeply in animism, and so the challenge is to present the river, the forest, and the land as both a living body, and a powerful spirit. As a designer I want to create places that are self-perpetuating and memorable, but it is important to remember that they may also be sacred, and certainly have a life of their own.

Many of the elements in Nairobi River Park are directly related to the daily life and culture of East Africa, including trees used for timber, forage and fuel; a "Shamba Makula" (farm) for indigenous food and medicinal plants; Kenyan fodder and utility grasses; and the restoration of riverine forest. A "sculpture garden," perpetually in progress, consists of contemporary and future carving trees; and a "Shamba Chakula" deals with issues of food and crops. Other areas are concerned with ethnobotany, economic plantations (exports), and the landscape history of Nairobi. The farm-gardens will provide food and jobs to people who need them, and using traditional native artists and craftspeople to build the bridges, paths, and seating (all either literal, or contemporary reinterpretations of ancient materials and techniques), will add another level of both employment and cultural uniqueness.

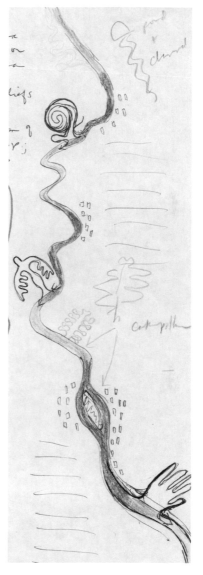

Nairobi River Park is especially concerned with environmental education and so historical and cultural values are integrated with recreating and cleansing whole ecosystems. Target food and habitat plantings for specific birds, butterflies, waterfowl, baboons, and monkeys occur along the shoreline. The centerpiece of the ecosystem, however, is the river itself, which from the beginning has been treated as a sewer, and development has added industrial effluent (including caustic soda, lime, bleaching agents, and unknown by-products) to the human and animal wastes that pollute the system. People who cannot afford to buy water drink from the river, and numerous children die every year from related diseases.

Thus, a major component of the park is a series of environmental sculptures...whose primary purpose is water purification. The images in the sculptures– snake, snail, bird, caterpillar, human hand– are universal symbols associated with regeneration and the living world, and the configurations are placed alongside existing bodies of polluted water. The forms themselves, constructed as long, narrow, meandering channels and shallow wetland ponds, range from two to three feet deep, and are thickly-planted with aquatic vegetation (bulrushes, cattails, reeds, and sedges) and filled with microorganisms such that suspended solids sink to the bottom and are decomposed by bacteria. Water is diverted into these natural filtering systems ("functional sculptures") whenever pollution becomes dangerous, and cleansed water is returned to the river after its "journey of purification."

– Patricia Johanson, 1996 (a)

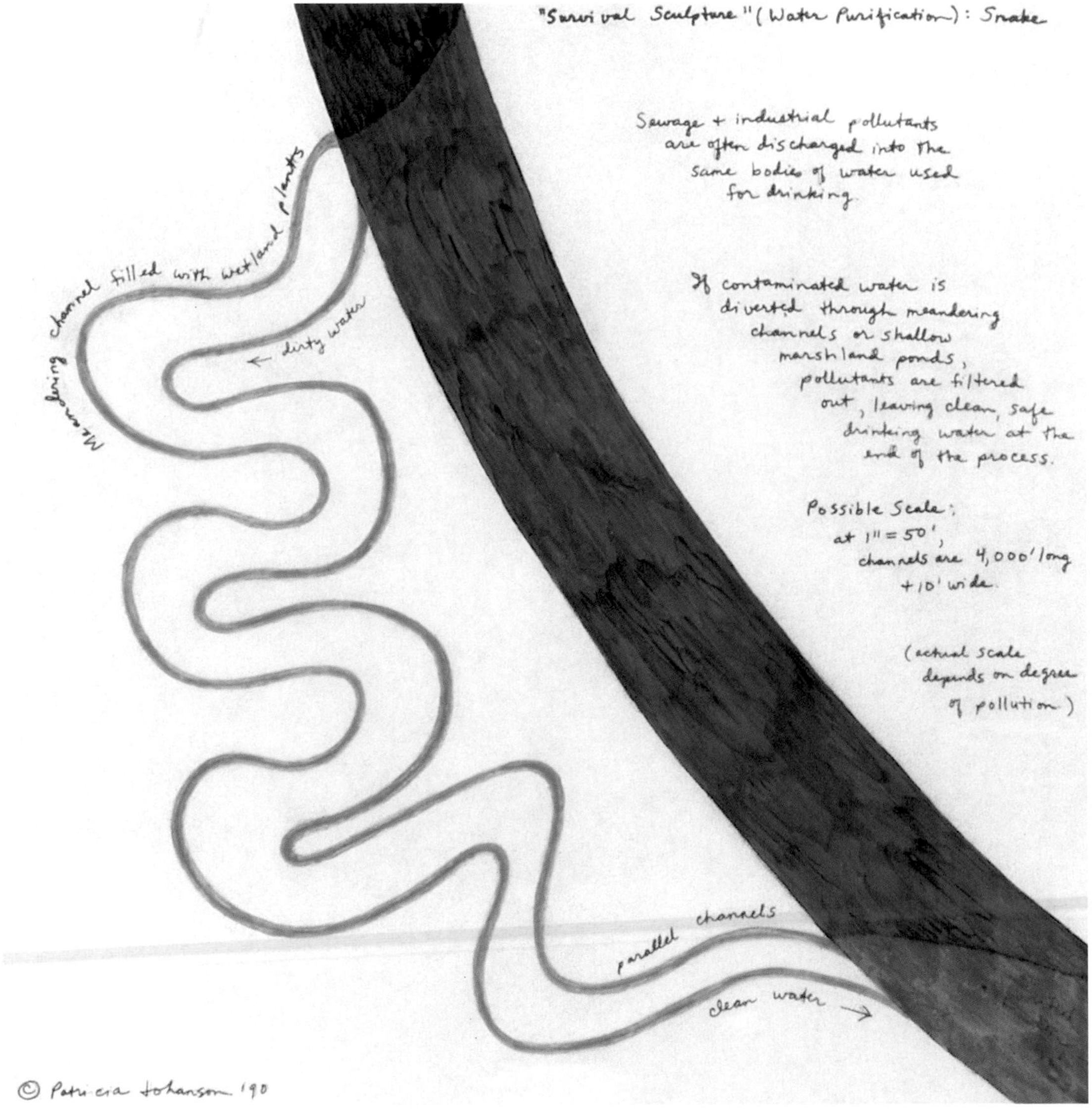

"Survival Sculpture" (Water Purification): Snake

Sewage + industrial pollutants
are often discharged into the
same bodies of water used
for drinking.

If contaminated water is
diverted through meandering
channels or shallow
marshland ponds,
pollutants are filtered
out, leaving clean, safe
drinking water at the
end of the process.

Possible Scale:
at 1" = 50',
channels are 4,000' long
+ 10' wide.

(actual scale
depends on degree
of pollution)

Meandering channel filled with wetland plants

← dirty water

parallel channels

clean water →

© Patricia Johanson '90

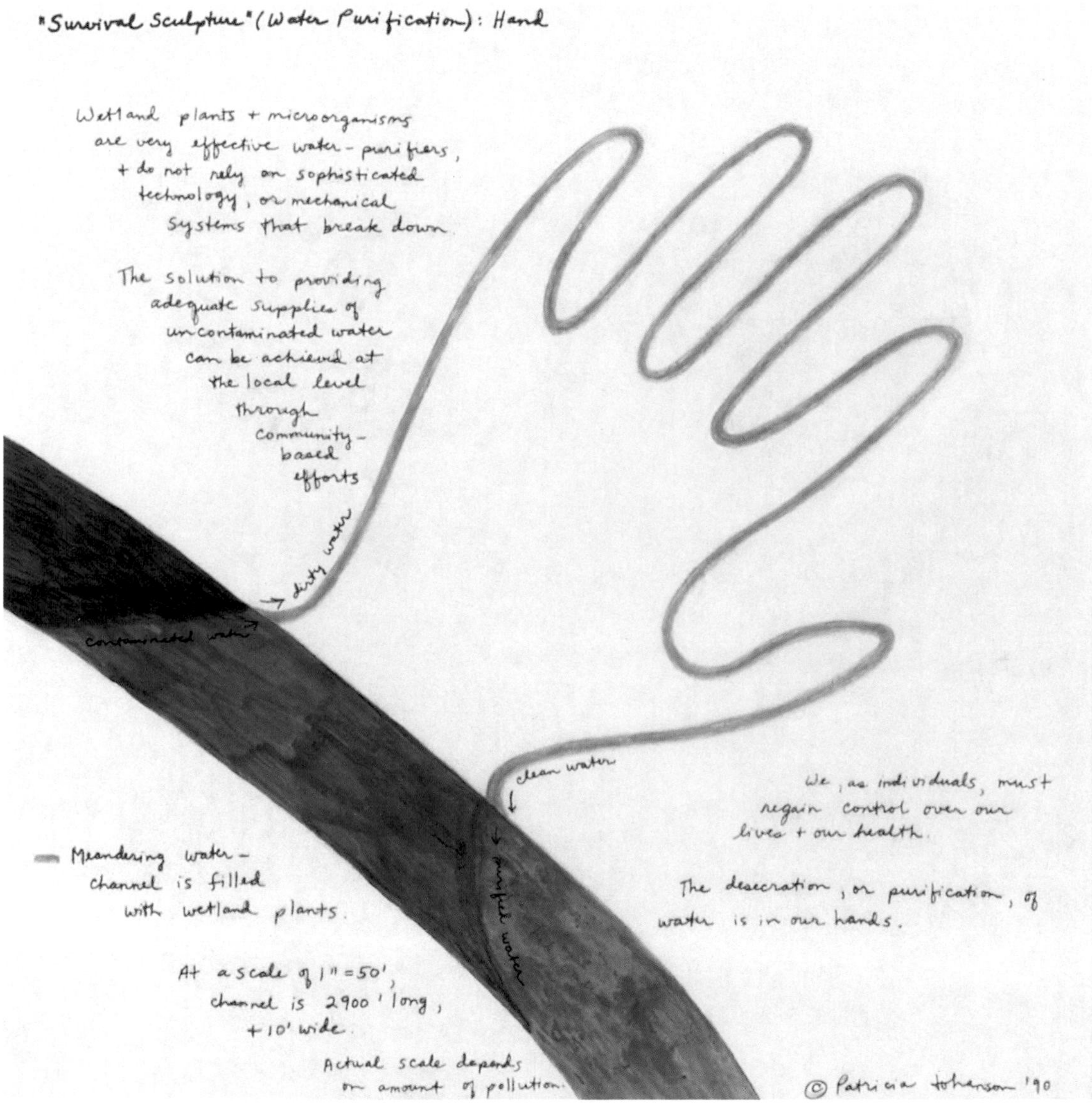

"Survival Sculpture" (Water Purification): Hand

Wetland plants + microorganisms
are very effective water-purifiers,
+ do not rely on sophisticated
technology, or mechanical
systems that break down.

The solution to providing
adequate supplies of
uncontaminated water
can be achieved at
the local level
through
community-
based
efforts

dirty water

contaminated water

clean water

clean water

Meandering water-
channel is filled
with wetland plants.

At a scale of 1" = 50',
channel is 2900' long,
+ 10' wide.

Actual scale depends
on amount of pollution.

We, as individuals, must
regain control over our
lives + our health.

The desecration, or purification, of
water is in our hands.

© Patricia Johanson '90

huge problems in infrastructure projects. Johanson began developing *Survival Sculptures* in the city of Nairobi. She describes the Nairobi River as "totally polluted, with bodies of animals, industrial chemicals, raw sewage and waste from slaughter-houses floating by." She saw people who were forced to draw their drinking water from the contaminated river, noting that "a typical slum, such as Majengo, with a population density of 56,000 per square kilometer, has no water connections, no sewer or drainage systems, no roads, no garbage disposal and no health care."[6]

Johanson was interested in developing the *Survival Sculptures* as a community project, related to the National Museum of Kenya, Nairobi River ecology, Kenyan craftspeople and jobs. She planned to use local weavers to create bridges across the river. She designed space for a sculpture garden to be carved out of living trees by local artists. River Wardens were planned as guides for Nairobi River Park through a museum-based education program. While she worked on the project in Africa during the 1990s, the political situation in Kenya deteriorated and Nairobi became increasingly unsafe. The project has now been suspended.

While the *Survival Sculptures* are appealingly simple, another of Johanson's current projects is remarkably multi-layered and complex. *Ulsan Park* is a 912-acre ecological park under construction in Korea. In 1996, she and other major landscape designers from around the world were invited to participate in a visioning process for the park by oil refining giant Yukong Ltd. Before their arrival, participants were given site information and technical research, along with the park program and goals. Yukong operates the largest petroleum refinery in the world in the industrial city of Ulsan. The company wanted the park – their gift to the citizens of the city – to become the world's major ecological park of the 21st century.

After a week of discussion, research and site visits, the designers presented potential schematic plans for the park. Johanson immediately saw that the dragon – which is found throughout Korean art – could be a unifying image. "The dragon is frequently depicted emerging from clouds or water, so you see fragments of the image, but not the whole thing," she says. "This seemed a perfect analogy for *Ulsan Park*, because we had only scraps of accessible landscape. Because of the topography, none of it was continuous. You would walk up the valley, and it would dead-end. You would be on the ridge of a mountain, looking down, but you couldn't get anywhere from there. But we had water and sky –and the dragon is the mediator between them." Her initial Master Plan for *Ulsan Park* scattered dragon imagery throughout the site, unifying hiking trails, exhibition halls, restaurants and playgrounds with waterways and microhabitats.

Johanson was asked to remain in Korea to work on the design for the park with the landscape firm Oikos and the Yukong team. Over a six-week period she detailed ecological playgrounds to teach children about water, forests and agriculture, native habitat for specific species interwoven with public facilities, and a *Dragon Trail* of linked gardens along the crest of the mountains. This enormous project is composed of numerous smaller parts, including a *Tiger Paw Spillway*, *Carp Playground* and *Dragon Eye/Cloud Garden*. The pattern of mountains and valleys frame public spaces. Johanson's design reconnects the flow of disrupted water—which she describes as "the life force of the site." She adds: "The psychological key to my design was to restore living ecological communities that would sustain the beloved, but threatened, plant and animal guardians of Korean mythology. I wanted to establish a resonance between local landscape and inner beliefs."[7] The park contains habitat for tigers, deer, cranes, waterfowl, bats, fish and insects. *Ulsan Park* consists of at least fifteen different projects placed within a matrix of landscape and culture, unified by the image of the Dragon.

With quiet certainty, Johanson advances a new cultural paradigm. She uses the rich personal creativity allowed by the historical separation of art from life in useful service to nature and society. Since the Industrial Revolution, art has been traded as a commodity with no social function apart from its monetary value. Suzi Gablik writes: "If any social function can be ascribed to ... art ..., it is the function to have no function."[8] The separation of art from common necessity and social existence has led to an extraordinary flourishing of individual creativity. When a work of art no longer exists as a useful object or a social communication, it becomes a location where an artist's private meanings and individual genius can be expressed. Art turns into free space in which thought and invention are possible. Johanson does not abjure that freedom so

Above left: *Ulsan Park* site of *Dragon Eye Garden*

Right: *Ulsan Park*, Korea, *Dragon's Eye (Meditation Garden/Cloud Garden/Sunset Garden/Bat Garden)* (detail), 1996

Facing page left: *Ulsan Dragon Park*, Korea: *Tiger Tail Plaza*, 26" x 40½", colored pencil and ink, 1996

Right: *Ulsan Park* existing reservoir, site of the *Tiger-Stripe Marsh and Paw spillway*

Ulsan Dragon Park, South Korea, 1996-2005

Ulsan Dragon Park occupies 912 acres in the middle of Korea's leading industrial city, home of Hyundai, shipbuilding, Pohang Steel, and the largest oil refinery in the world, Yukong, Ltd., the donor of the park. The Korean people traditionally loved and worshipped nature, so the challenge is to combine Korea's agrarian, shamanistic past with its high-tech industrialized future, while also serving the recreational needs of a million people and creating a sustainable environment. The park program requires many major built structures—a city museum,

exhibition complexes, promenade, and Imax Theater—all interwoven with restored natural ecosystems: marsh, pond, intermittent creek, floodplain, meadows, wetland and upland forests....

Many elements in the park function simultaneously as art, cultural symbol, habitat and utilitarian structure .... A *Carp Playground* consists of a series of fish-scale terraces that flow from the mountainside down to the floodplain. A rivulet, manually activated by pumps, waterwheels, and sluice gates teaches children about water management as they fill reservoirs and wading pools and build tiny cities of pebbles and sand. At

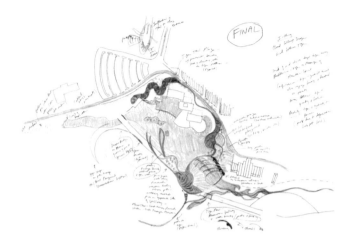

the bottom of the play terraces are narrow paths that lead through wetland planting, vernal pools, and a variety of floodplain microhabitats, such as amphibian breeding grounds.

... The educational program at Ulsan Park is centered around such issues as the survival of species, biodiversity, and the sustainable use of water, forests, energy, and agricultural land. To Korean people, the concept of longevity has great significance, therefore gardens devoted to such longevity symbols as turtle, crane, deer, pine and bamboo are designed to be not only poetic and deeply enmeshed in the cultural psyche, but also create

ecosystems where these plants and animals can survive.

Perhaps the most powerful symbol in the park is the dragon, an enormous image that appears in fragments throughout the site, uniting wetlands, valleys and mountaintops with the more urban areas of the park.... Koreans have always understood the dragon as a mediator between heaven and earth—the Celestial Dragon and the Water Dragon— responsible for rain and agriculture as well as bountiful sea harvests. Contemporary ecological thinking also envisions the flow of energy between water, air and earth; thus the dragon

becomes a metaphor for the elements and processes of nature, its cycles of production, decomposition and transformation.

When water was worshipped in Korea as the sacred sustainer of life, water pollution was not a problem. Perhaps by reintegrating nature and culture within public landscapes, we can ensure the transmission of both ancestral truths and the preservation of the gene pool that ceaselessly provides new forms, meanings and products.

– Patricia Johanson, 1997

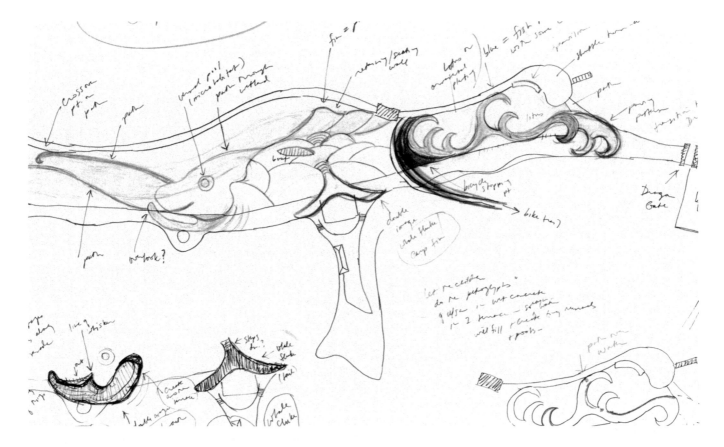

that art becomes some dreary form of social service. With her visionary projects and multiple goals, she creates trajectories along which individual creativity can flourish, while linked with social and environmental concerns.

NOTES:

1 Johanson, 1969, "Gardens that nourish, drift and transform .... the water garden."

2 A. Lipton, in S. Spaid, 2002, *Ecovention: Current Art to Transform Ecologies*, Cincinnati: the Contemporary Arts Center, p. 147.

3 Johanson, Summer 2003.

4 R. Morris, Spring 1980, "Notes on Art as/and Reclamation," October, no. 12, pp. 97-102, in J. Kastner and B. Wallis, Eds., 1998, *Land and Environmental Art*, New York: Phaidon, p. 255.

5 McDonough is the subject of a 2001 film, *The Next Industrial Revolution*, directed by C. Bedford and S. Morhaim.

6 Johanson, 1996 (a).

7 For further information see Johanson, 1997.

8 S. Gablik, 1995, *Conversations Before the End of Time*, London: Thames & Hudson, p. 248

Ulsan Dragon Park, Korea: Carp to Dragon (Water Terraces), 26" x 37", colored pencil and ink, 1996

Snake patterns fall apart as water enters the park. Run-off from rainwater or melting snow flows down drainage channels around a sunken room. The flooded room becomes a swimming-pool in summer / ice-skating in winter, with a color-island isolated from the shore. As the pool overflows, a "path" becomes a "stream", with gold platforms as "stepping stones", like patterns of river-ice, with water flowing below. Water washing over the colors creates new color-compositions. Overflow basins; rivulets, water-steps, fish, turtle + muskrat ponds are scattered throughout the park, adding sound, life, + echoes of the colors seen under water. The colors nature — grass, fish, willows, maples, + virgilia, with its silvery bark + silver leaves that turn yellow in the fall, reverberate in a magical landscape.

SITE PLAN: "Ulsan Dragon Park", Korea   © Patricia Johnson - 1996

SETTING THE MIND IN MOTION

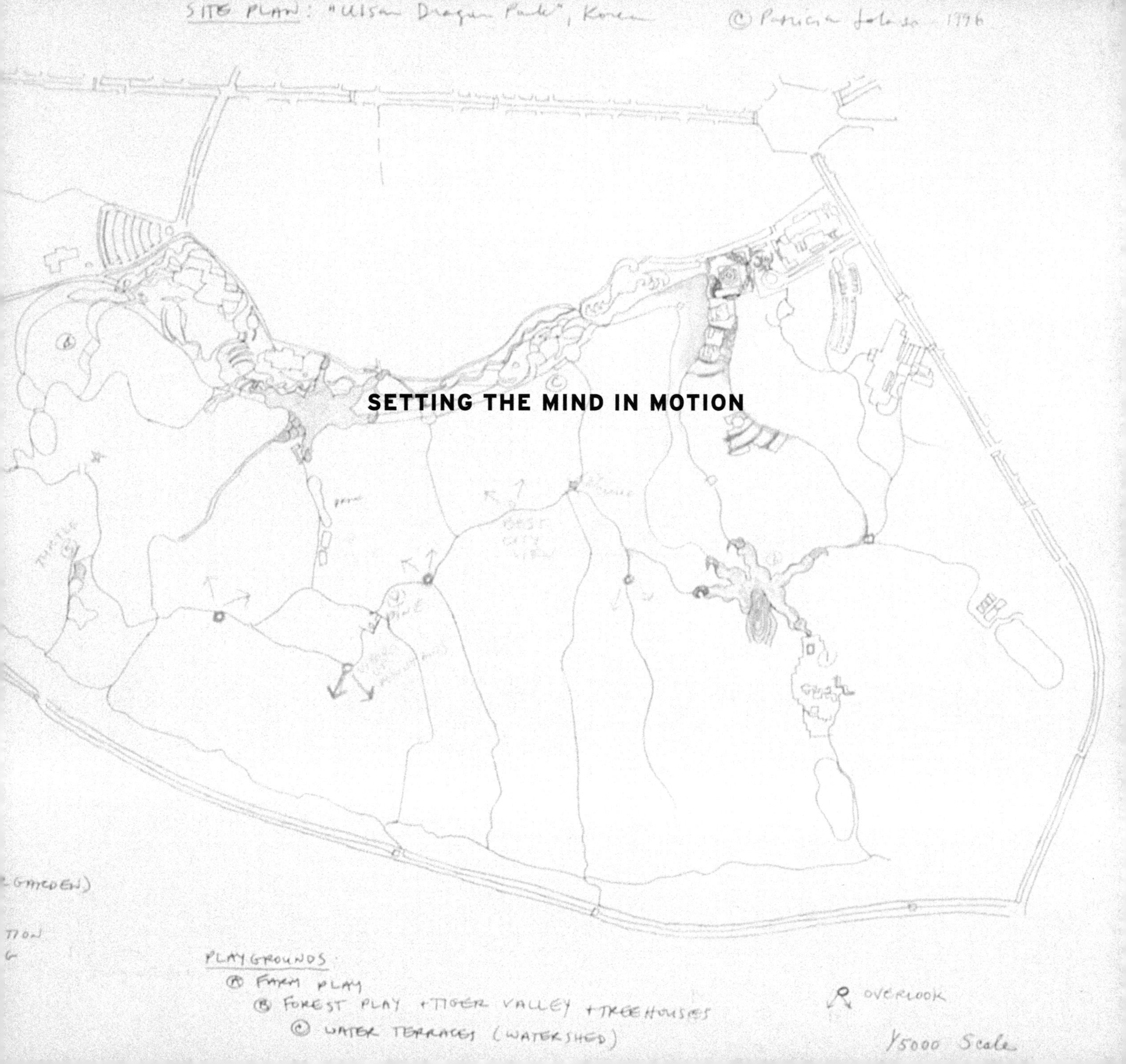

PLAYGROUNDS:
   (A) FARM PLAY
   (B) FOREST PLAY + TIGER VALLEY + TREEHOUSES
   (C) WATER TERRACES (WATERSHED)

overlook

1/5000 Scale

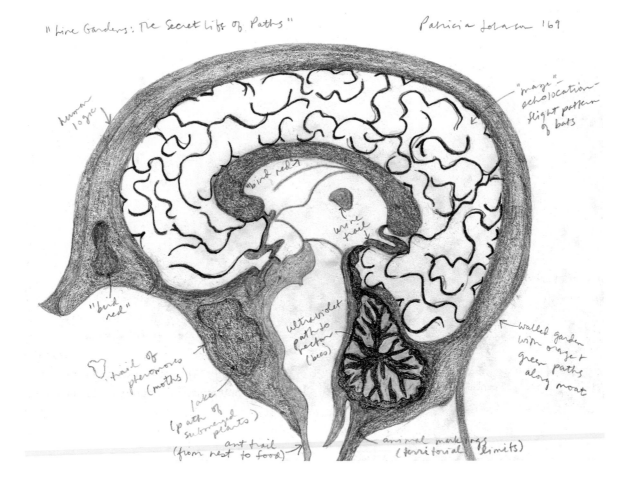

"Line Gardens: The Secret Life of Paths"   Patricia Johanson '69

human logic

"maze"
echolocation-
flight pattern
of bats

"bird red"

urine trail

"bird red"

trail of pheromones (moths)

ultraviolet path to nectar (bees)

lake (path of submerged plants)

ant trail (from nest to food)

animal markings (territorial limits)

walled garden with orange green paths along moat

SETTING THE MIND IN MOTION

Previous pages, left: *Snake in the Grass for Philip Glass: Pattern of Water* (detail), acrylic, ink and gouache, 42" x 69", 1985

Right: *Ulsan Dragon Park, Korea: Site Plan* (detail), ink and colored pencil, 18" x 39", 1996

Facing page: *Line Gardens: The Secret Life of Paths*, 8½" x 11", pencil and colored pencil, 1969

IN HER 1969 DRAWING, *ILLUSORY GARDEN: CORNFIELD*, JOHANSON NOTES: "A diagonal path – blatant enough to be noticed, but not interfering with farm machinery – draws one into the cornfield. Gradually the path narrows down to nothing and you are left alone in the cornfield." The design draws visitors into an ordinary – but largely unexplored – agricultural landscape, where it abandons them to their own observations, thoughts, fears and pleasures. Another design, *Field of Grass – Big Bluestem*, proposes a similar journey. Johanson notes on the drawing: "The person's body is engulfed by grass, over six feet high, as he moves along a narrow, winding path. The sense of 'no design' gives way to the details of grass, its interaction with sunlight and wind, and the chirps of insects and birds." The path arrives at a sunken, meditative space with glass walls allowing "the contemplation of nature's substructure – a forest of roots and harvester ants." Johanson's early drawings posit the visitors' encounter with a living landscape as the "work" of art. The artist's creation is designed to disappear as the visitor is engulfed by an encounter with nature. "By suspending objective, measurable space in favor of myriad detail, one arrives at a garden of effects and personal freedom," she writes. "Illusory Gardens are designed to provide inner renewal – to stimulate memory and fantasy by reaching out to our past, present and future selves."[1]

In other *House and Garden* drawings, Johanson explores the possibility of secret gardens, whose design can only be grasped through an imaginative act. *The Secret Life of Paths* is composed of overlapping trails created through invisible marks – pheromones, ultraviolet and urine – that draw the shape of a human brain. Other gardens use discontinuous forms to create very large-scale designs interwoven with nature. Some propose elements set so far apart that it would never be possible to see more than one element at a time. The image and meanings of such works must be pieced together in a viewer's mind and memory. In her essay on "Vanishing Point Gardens," Johanson writes that "one of the advantages of such a scheme is that it would require little (if any) destruction of the existing landscape. The design of a Vanishing Point Garden could be superimposed on any scene; however at no point would it be possible to see the total design – in fact it would never even be possible to see any two elements in relation to each other. Each part would be discrete, isolated – existing only in the context of its own surroundings."[2]

More than twenty years later, Johanson used these strategies to create a *Master Plan for Rockland County, New York* (1990), where she proposed using cumulative experience and a mental image to create an art that would frame and interpret the existing world. Johanson describes her plan: "The county is 175 square miles, so the design cannot be seen from an airplane or helicopter – it exists only as an image in the mind. The image becomes a trail, and the trail occurs along existing roads. There is nothing added except the mental image, which becomes a map that both links and leads people to all the extraordinary sites in the county."

The mental image is also key to Johanson's 1984 design for *Pelham Bay Park*, New York, a sculpture aimed at increasing the visibility of the tides. "The 'image' is really a series of images in constant flux – metaphorical fragments – so that the mind of the spectator plays as much of a role as the water in shaping the piece," she writes. "Stepped basins in the center retain the water after the tide is out as a 'memory' or reminder of water having been there. This sense of connections continuously broken and renewed is a major part of the aesthetic."[3]

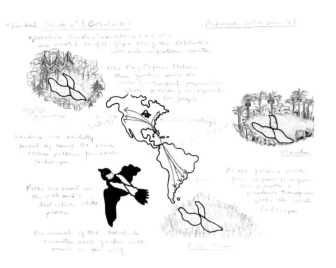

Public Art Master Plan, Rockland County, New York, 1989-91

The goal of the *Public Art Master Plan* has been not only to identify a preliminary group of sites that might be suitable for large-scale environmental art, but also to link those sites to Rockland County's significant patterns– social, histori-cal, cultural, and natural. Landscape has played a major role, because topography is a major determinant of historical, social, cultural, and commercial interactions....

The plan for the Rockland Trail would be overlaid on existing roads – those persistent trackways – using the image to explore a range of significant places, with the idea that familiar places would become more comprehensible, while new discoveries would be made.

– Patricia Johanson, 1991

Top: *Linked Gardens (Bobolink)*, 8½" x 11", pencil, ink and colored pencil, 1969

Bottom: *Public Art Master Plan, Rockland County*, New York, 11" x 8½", colored pencil, ink and typewriting on printed plan, 1991

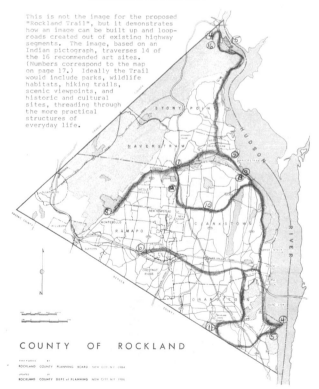

DEMONSTRATION SCHEMATIC IMAGE

This is not the image for the proposed "Rockland Trail", but it demonstrates how an image can be built up and loop-roads created out of existing highway segments. The image, based on an Indian pictograph, traverses 14 of the 16 recommended art sites. (Numbers correspond to the map on page 17.) Ideally the Trail would include parks, wildlife habitats, hiking trails, scenic viewpoints, and historic and cultural sites, threading through the more practical structures of everyday life.

COUNTY OF ROCKLAND

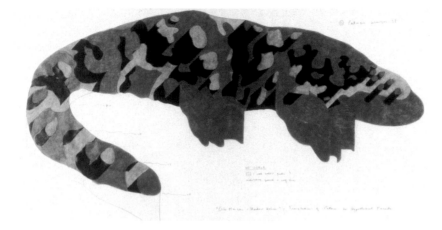

Tidal Sculpture Garden, Pelham Bay Park, New York City, 1984, project dimensions: 540' x 300' x 12' high

To posit working with the tides is both romantic and technically challenging, with unforeseen results the only certainty, and yet predictability is hardly a value an artist should have to worry about. The major aim of this sculpture is to increase the visibility of the tides– the poetry and drama of the coming and going of the water…. On its simplest level, the incoming tide is routed through a series of spaces to form an ever-expanding pattern. The image (a "flower") is actually an abstract maze of walls, which in turn become "spillways" as the water overflows each compartment. The walls themselves are sculptural…. To as great an extent as possible they should have that organic, erratic quality of natural forms– the sense of having been formed and deformed in response to natural forces….At high tide all that would be left is an island (the "bud"). As water flows out, the sculpture would gradually be revealed, and the sunken garden would once again become walkable.

– Patricia Johanson, 1985

Left: *Gila Monster-Shadow House, Translation of Pattern to Hypothetical Façade*, 30" x 60", ink, charcoal and conte crayon, 1978. Collection: Museum of Modern Art, New York. Acquired with Matching Funds from Mr. and Mrs. Richard Deutsch and the National Endowment for the Arts

Right: *Tidal Sculpture Garden, Orchard Beach, New York, Site Plan*, 36" x 24", ink and charcoal, 1984

With art that can only be seen and grasped through an imaginative act, Johanson sets the mind in motion. In this work, she is inspired by ancient geoglyphs, like the Nazca Lines in Peru. These enormous images, formed by removing a top layer of desert pavement to expose a lighter soil, were created between 200 BCE and 700 CE. Their purpose is mysterious, and the method through which they were constructed indecipherable, as the images can only be seen from mountaintops and airplanes. These designs were probably experienced through ritual walking, while focused attention allowed the image to accumulate in mind and memory. The Great Serpent Mound, found in Adams County, Ohio, winds for over 1300 feet along the edge of a bluff. This huge effigy mound was painstakingly built circa 200 BCE with clay carried up from the valley below. Like other effigy mounds and giant earth images, such as the White Horse of Uffington in England, the Great Serpent Mound obviates the one-point perspective of a single spectator. It is addressed beyond the eye, to earth and sky, and human capacities for imagination and spirit. Cave paintings of antiquity, hidden in darkness, with their multiple viewpoints and overlapping images, also suggest an art designed to set the mind in motion.

In a 1985 essay written for *The Princeton Journal*, Johanson describes precedents for her art in the cave paintings of Altimira, where "the paintings literally become the topography of the cave." In Anasazi cliff dwellings, she finds something akin to the "fusion" of building and site she seeks in her own designs. When asked about her influences, Johanson cites these artifacts of ancient cultures, where she finds a synthesis of culture and nature.

Johanson concludes her 1969 essay "Gardens by the Mile... Line Gardens" with the startling proposition that "The viewer becomes the artist. The sculpture becomes the place." Western art since the time of the Renaissance can be described as oriented to a single spectator and expressing the view of a single artist. Johanson suggests an alternate paradigm. With an art so large and so interwoven with a specific place and its myriad details, people must physically explore an environment to experience the work. Johanson says "Projects like *Philip Glass*, *Tidal Gardens*, and *Rainforest Park* depend heavily on the physical involvement of the visitor. They need to explore. Each person

"Flower Fountain" (Drowned Landscape)
Pattern of Land & Water at "High Tide"

© Katrich Johnson '82

yellow sandstone
water
ground cover
trees

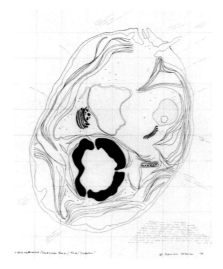

sees different patterns, and has their own experiences. It becomes a personal journey. The transformations are occurring both outside and within ourselves." Everyone experiences a project differently, and each individual's imagination, thoughts, aspirations and meanings are given space within the work. No specific perspective, orientation or focal point is assumed. Each person moving through the form decides what to look at. The viewer becomes the center of the work.

Johanson writes of her projects, "The ... structures, seemingly arbitrary and erratic, are usually large-scale versions of life forms that inhabit each particular place. Their peculiarity invites exploration, and within a less anthropomorphic setting, such as the forest, they offer a comforting human presence, luring the visitor in. The forms are usually discovered to be purposeful, even if not understood, which adds another layer of mystery and further impetus for investigation. Movement through the garden depends on variable and shifting individual circumstances, thus the creativity of both landscape and viewer are incorporated into the design."[4]

Multiple layers, hidden structures and worlds within worlds characterize Johanson's designs. It is a way of working she learned from studying plants. One of the *Plant Drawings for Projects* she completed in 1974 is based on a microscopic green algae. Titled *Chlamydomonas/Landscape Design/Park/Sculpture*, the drawing translates a single-celled plant into a walled park, using the forms of the plant to delineate terracing and climbing structures, pavilions, pools and fountains. Johanson notes that *Chlamydomonas* "is a complex, highly-organized miniature world." The multi-layered image invites viewers to make an imaginative leap from microscopic to macroscopic, local to global, separate individuality to connected community.

Facing page: *Flower Fountain-Drowned Landscape, Pattern of Land and Water at High Tide*, 36" x 42", acrylic, ink, gouache and pastel, 1982

Above: *Chlamydomonas/Landscape Design/Park/Sculpture*, 30" x 24", ink, 1974

Johanson's work engages unconscious perceptions and visceral responses. One of her 1969 *House and Garden* designs, *Garden of Ghosts*, is generated by ground fog. Grassy meadows and bowl-shaped topography, conducive to the formation of fog, are traversed by tiny metal grate paths over natural drainage channels. On the drawing she writes, "The garden becomes foggier as you descend into it (if fear doesn't prevent descent)." She imagines people walking through "a wonderland of strange forms" in the "cold and damp of moisture-saturated air." This is a garden of mystery, where visitors find their way with intuition and caution, drawing on faith, and perhaps fearing the loss of control.

According to Johanson: "The brain is still largely a mystery. I have studied it throughout my career, trying to figure out how to make more powerful art. I understand that everything we perceive as 'out there' is really occurring inside our heads. Different

Facing page left:
O'Keeffe/Equivalents-Color Garden/Sculpture/Park, Patterns of Color, 54" x 36", acrylic, ink and pastel, 1985. Collection of The Berkshire Museum, Pittsfield, Massachusetts

Right: *O'Keeffe/Equivalents-Color Garden/Sculpture/Park, Topographical Overlay*, 54" x 36", conte crayon, pastel, charcoal and ink, 1985. Collection of The Berkshire Museum

This page: *O'Keeffe/Equivalents-Color Garden/Sculpture/Park, Plan*, 54" x 36", ink and charcoal, 1985. Collection of The Berkshire Museum

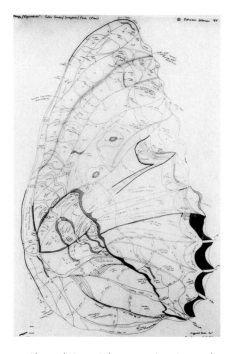

human heads harbor different information, just as different creatures perceive the world differently. Our physical equipment, needs, values and survival strategies all determine how we see and what we pay attention to." Johanson speaks of aiming at visceral and emotional resonances rather than intellectual responses, so that the art is experienced not merely aesthetically, but also biologically and physically. "I have always believed that people like my work not because of what they consciously 'see,' but rather because of what they subconsciously perceive. I try to tap into people's unconscious and subconscious emotions, and powerful universal experiences, by using cues within the design."

In *O'Keeffe Equivalents*, 1985 designs for earth-sculpture, Johanson aims to produce a landscape of intimate, interwoven spaces. The topography is based on fragmented body images of Georgia O'Keeffe, taken from photographs by Alfred Stieglitz, interwoven with the color patterns of a butterfly. A third overlay allows for park accoutrements. "By superimposing many different ways of looking at the same thing – a tangled web of multiple meanings – viewing the work becomes a creative, intuitive experience," Johanson writes.[5] As visitors physically explore aesthetic and ecological layers, experiencing wind, weather, and their own thoughts and interests at any given moment, they move deeper into the project. "These hidden layers make the work more powerful. They also free the mind, allowing it to go backwards and forward in time."

Johanson uses the image of "nested dolls" as a metaphor for her work. "What I really want in all my projects – and how I approach things – is to go deeper and deeper." If

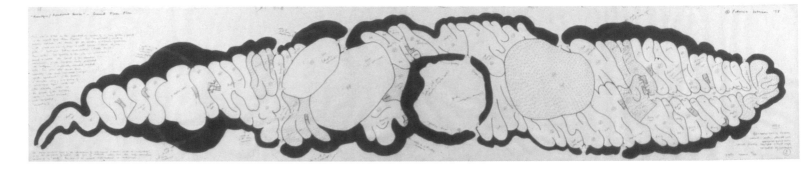

132

people are engaged by the monumental image and become intrigued enough to explore it, they will discover within it an intricate layering of images, events and meanings. "You get layers of living ecologies, the history of the place, ephemeral effects and personal meanings. These layers of experience go on and on."

Building and living with *Cyrus Field*, Johanson realized that designs incorporating nature engage viewers in restructured relationships with the world around them. In a talk she gave at the dedication of *Fair Park Lagoon* in 1986, she said "the problem is to establish feelings of connectedness, while setting the mind free to dream.... Because the landscape is simultaneously large and small – a tangled web of myriad detail and expansive, radiant space – it offers the possibility of dialogue and personal connections."[6] She sees the meaning of the work as constituted through both conscious and subliminal connections made by each visitor, as formal and accidental correspondences that resonate in the brain. She cites as an example the actual snakes that are often seen at *Cyrus Field* and innumerable serpentine rivulets of water occurring around and within the sculpture. As these patterns mirror each other at different scales, they offer a glimpse of some deeper natural truth. Johanson writes: "Physical exploration is the key and uncharted territory is the goal, as each individual visitor moves at his own pace, toward his own meaning, within a garden of infinite detail."[7]

Mountain Apartment House, Ground Floor Plan, 15" x 75", ink and charcoal, 1978. Collection of University Galley, University of Massachusetts at Amherst, gift of Ira Sahlman, New York

In the late 1970s, Johanson designed a series of buildings as landscapes. *Estuary/Maze House* is a plan for a dwelling sunk into the ground and surrounded by water, so that it becomes like a tidal estuary with a low-relief network of creeks and marshes. A vast, elaborate design for a *Child's Geology House* translates a glacial valley, cliffs, canyons, volcano, flood basalt, subterranean caves and the continental shelf into details of a park, museum and playhouse. With such "modest proposals," Johanson explores the possibility of an invisible architecture. Describing these plans as works where "'structure' is dissolved,"[8] she writes: "Traditionally we speak of building and site as two separate entities. There is 'sensitive site planning' and occasionally an interpenetration of house and garden, but never a *fusion* of the two." Johanson follows nature's design strategy, which incorporates growth and change, history and suffering. She notes that this is "diametrically opposed to the drawing board approach." She continues, "Real landscapes are rugged; sensual; muddy; ordinary; inaccessible. They are filled with things that are dead, overgrown and imperfect – things that are [too young and][9] too old. But they have life and are interesting because they are not perfect, and because unexpected things happen...." She suggests that art, architecture, landscape and planning can be reinvented by incorporating this vitality, imperfection, and unpredictability. Instead of creating intimidating forms devoid of real power, artists and architects "can expand outward into structures with value and meaning for the 'real' world – both natural and human."

For Johanson, immersion in a natural landscape is what allows for "the primacy of the person." Meanings become multiple and change with the viewer. Instead of presenting visitors with a dictatorial form and function, forms and meanings can change, age, contradict and evolve. She writes, "The tranquility of landscape – its restorative power – has to do with this blurring of boundaries, the capacity for change, the offering of choices, and the possibility of finding ourselves within it."[10] She calls on creative people to design the way nature does, building open-ended structures that contain myriad other structures within them.

In the 1970s, Johanson wrote an article for *Heresies Magazine* called "Women's Traditional Arts: Organizing the Scraps." In it she explored the creativity of women making home, meals, quilts, gardens and garments out of scraps that remain. The article was never published. Johanson wonders if the editors preferred to focus on women's success in culturally authoritative spheres and male-defined terms. Johanson has always felt more connected with everyday aspects of women's creative language and processes. Like a quiltmaker, her patient stitches connect scraps in an unexpected aesthetic statement that is useful and life-sustaining. Working in the realm of parks and infrastructure projects – connecting remnant ecosystems, habitats, watersheds and recreation corridors – Johanson engages this tradition.

"The whole idea of 'organizing the scraps' has been very important to me. I used to watch my grandmother cook. She would empty the shelves and find two scoops of this and one of that, and prepare a gourmet meal out of whatever she had on hand. It's that kind of analogy – you need to use everything; you don't throw things out. The scraps are what you make the great work out of. They stimulate your creativity. It's a tradition I really admire. Combining art and infrastructure with the living landscape involves figuring out how all the parts that don't logically go together can be connected. It is very much like a patchwork quilt. How do you organize it all so everything is enhancing everything else?"

"If you think about connecting up habitats and watersheds while building recreational corridors, that's certainly 'organizing the scraps.' Given all the shopping malls, developments, housing projects and transportation corridors, what's left? They are remnants, but they can be woven into something magnificent. I think the patchwork quilt is a good analogy for large-scale design."

Throughout her career, Johanson has created a body of ideas that challenge and empower people to change their attitudes, free their minds and transform the world around them. Often with a simple drawing, made on a letter-sized sheet of paper, she presents radical ideas that spark social activism and environmental change. "My typical drawing is on a sheet of typing paper," she says. "I just start faxing it to everybody and saying, 'What about this?' I did that in Petaluma. I made a sketch that defined the sewage treatment areas, tidal wetlands, and recreational zonation – all within the image of the butterfly. By looking at this simple drawing, you could begin to see the

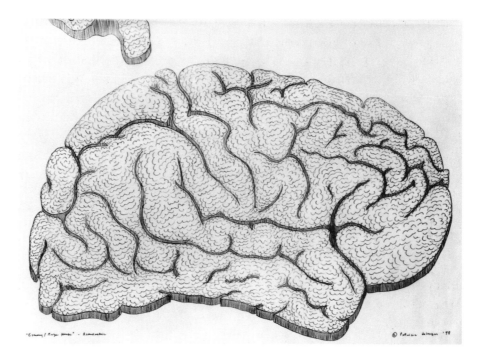

"Estuary / Maze House" - Axonometric   © Patricia Johanson '78

Estuary/Maze House: Axonometric,
30" x 42", conte crayon, 1978

possibilities." The drawing gives people a vision of what they can do over time. If they are excited by the ideas, they can pursue the opportunities. Johanson points out that it doesn't take money, support or marketing strategy to have ideas that set people's minds in motion.

Following her vision, Johanson has bridged barriers between art, architecture, landscape, planning and restoration ecology. She challenges each of these disciplines to expand beyond its narrow range of goals. She speaks of allowing natural processes to determine the forms of built structures and human communities, "so that people can dwell in a matrix of reconnected, self-sustaining and regenerative nature."[11] Her projects envision cooperative, human-made, living landscapes that ameliorate flooding, filter sewage, and restore biological richness, where neither nature nor culture is relegated to a decorative amenity. Johanson teaches that artists can be vital, visionary forces in creating social and environmental change.

Johanson's work creates spaces in which visitors' individuality and private meanings can flourish, while becoming connected with social significance and the world of nature. With rich, unusual environments that people experience at their own pace, over time, she asserts the possibility of places in which human beings and nature are not opposites. Inside a Johanson project or drawing, people attend to the unity and diversity of every form of life. They can stretch their minds and allow their creative capacities to unfold. Linking art and survival through multiple layers of image and meaning, Johanson's work invites us to change what we dream, transform how we see and revolutionize the ways we act in the world.

NOTES:

1 Johanson, 1969, "Gardens of the Senses and the Mind... Illusory Gardens."

2 Johanson, 1969, "Gardens that are Out of Sight...the Vanishing Point Garden."

3 Johanson, 1985, unpublished manuscript.

4 Johanson, 2000.

5 Johanson, 1986.

6 Johanson, 1986.

7 Johanson, 2003, p. 102.

8 Johanson, 1985, p. 110.

9 Johanson, 1985. Johanson adds this note by hand to the printed article. She writes, "It was in the original manuscript, but omitted in the printing." (Personal correspondence, 2004).

10 Johanson, 1985.

11 Johanson, 1988

Facing page: *Park for a Parking Garage*, 18½" x 26", ink and charcoal, 1986

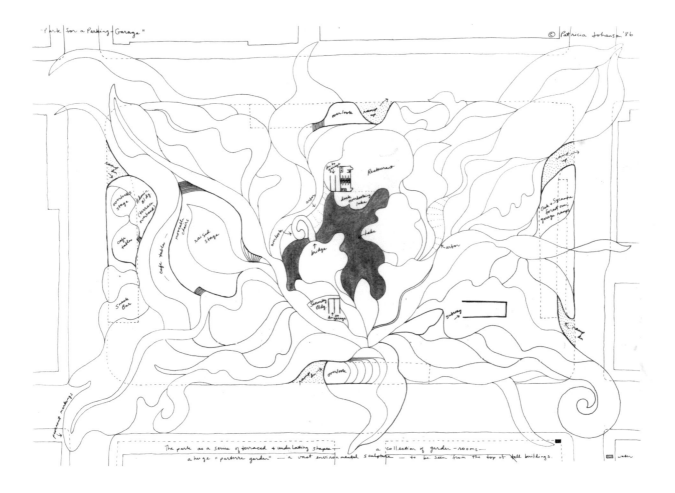

"Park for a Parking Garage" © Patricia Johanson '86

The park as a series of terraced & undulating shapes — a collection of garden-rooms —
a huge "parterre garden" — a vast environmental sculpture — to be seen from the top of tall buildings.

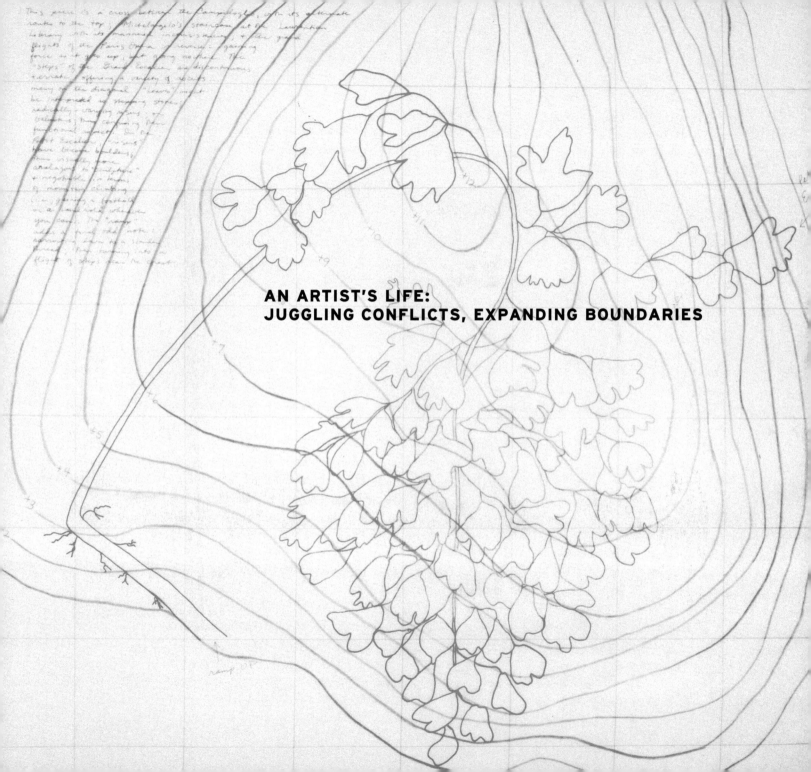

AN ARTIST'S LIFE:
JUGGLING CONFLICTS, EXPANDING BOUNDARIES

AN ARTIST'S LIFE:
JUGGLING CONFLICTS, EXPANDING BOUNDARIES

WHEN THE TIME CAME FOR PATRICIA JOHANSON TO APPLY TO COLLEGES, SHE HAD ONLY ONE ambition: to attend the Oberlin Conservatory of Music. But her mother feared that such a specialized education might be too confining for her headstrong, creative daughter. She urged Johanson to consider Bennington College, which had a unique program allowing students to design their own studies in Fine Arts. Since Bennington had a full music program, Johanson decided she could attend the college. From the day she arrived, it was a perfect fit. Johanson has blessed her mother every day since.

"I was obsessive about music, just like I was always obsessive about everything. I was the type of person who would wear the same dress every day. If I liked a certain food, I wanted to eat it every day. I never looked for variety. I found what I loved, and then wanted more of that." At Bennington, the Vermont landscape was beautiful and nourishing. In her classes, top caliber teachers – many of them artists – helped individual students follow their passions and achieve their goals.

Johanson wanted to take only music courses, but her academic advisor insisted she add one more thing. Johanson grudgingly signed up for a painting class. She laughs, remembering, "I just totally fell in love with it." Although she had always painted and

Previous pages, left: *Ixion's Wheel*, one of six truckloads arrives at State University of New York at Albany, 1969. Eugene Goossen, far left, Patricia Johanson, far right, truck driver and sons

Right: *Venus Maidenhair Fern/ Staircase/Ramp/Sculpture*, 24" x 24", ink and charcoal, 1974. Collection: Debra Bricker Balken

Facing page: Patricia Johanson pregnant, 1973 (photo: Ellsworth Kelly)

drawn, "suddenly I could make big paintings. Suddenly there was a dialogue. There were people who were taking my work seriously, and there was an art historical context I had never imagined. I didn't realize there was such a thing as art history! And there were real people doing this, professional careers. I started going to New York galleries and museums, and it changed my life. Eventually I dropped out of music, because I was so immersed in art."

Johanson (left) in 1961 with Helen Feeley, Helen Frankenthaler, and Lisa Motherwell

142

Between 1958 and 1962, Johanson learned about the monumental canvases of Abstract Expressionism. Andy Warhol's soup-can paintings were introduced as the "hot new thing" when she was in her senior year. Yet Johanson conceived and created large-scale, sculptural paintings that later became known as "Minimalist." At the time, her father worked with equipment for large ships where exterior canvas covers would occasionally be replaced. Johanson used the discarded canvases for her paintings. She laughs, "I would get these big, oddly-shaped gyroscope covers – they would be as large as a living room rug. All my paintings had a thick seam through the middle, and grommets along the edge." In her sophomore year, she conceived and constructed a series of *Color Rooms*. "A room is monumental, but it's also ready-made, internal space," she says. "I didn't need to go out and build something big. All I had to do was see the shapes, and where the different colors would go. I didn't spend a lot of money on materials. I used what was already there."

Johanson's originality excited her teachers, and they became her mentors and friends. One weekend when she was in New York City visiting galleries, she ran into her painting instructor, Paul Feeley. He invited his star pupil to meet Helen Frankenthaler.

"Of course my eyes lit up, because she was the great woman painter who had graduated from Bennington. We all aspired to be Helen Frankenthaler," Johanson recalls.

When Frankenthaler answered the door, Feeley grinned at her, pointed at Johanson, and said, "I'd like you to meet the next Helen Frankenthaler." Frankenthaler graciously welcomed the talented young student, and the two women became close companions.

Through Frankenthaler, and through Bennington's visiting speakers program, Johanson met many art-world luminaries of the day. She was invited to Clement Greenberg's New York City dinner parties after he came to speak at Bennington. She got to know David Smith when he came to the college to see one of her *Color Rooms*. Johanson knew Barnett Newman when she was a student, and later visited his apartment to see his new paintings, such as *The Stations of the Cross*. "Barney had very few exhibitions at that point," Johanson remembers. "He certainly was not universally admired." As a senior, Johanson spent her non-resident term in New York City working for Joseph Cornell.

Around this time Johanson fell in love with a Bennington art history professor, Eugene Goossen. Goossen was twenty years older than Johanson, and married. Johanson was stimulated by their intellectual companionship. Goossen promoted the idea of artists working on a gigantic scale, writing that "largeness.... [is] a necessary prerequisite...not to overpower the spectator, but to make him aware of an experience which can transcend a purely aesthetic emotion."[1] In these early years, Johanson found their relationship "both exciting and beneficial." Goossen was an art critic

Top: Johanson, Andre Emmerich and Eugene Goossen, c. 1964

Bottom: with photographer Hans Namuth, c. 1962

143

who was able to include her work in exhibits he curated. He was part of a social and intellectual context she enjoyed, while she also valued her independent life.

In 1960, Johanson met the visionary architect Frederick Kiesler when he came to speak at Bennington. Kiesler, who designed architecture that was really sculpture, had a profound impact on Johanson, and he also found a kindred spirit in her. When he learned that she was taking a secretarial job instead of pursuing her artwork during a non-resident term, he insisted that she paint instead. He gave her his studio at 59 East Ninth Street in New York for the winter of 1961, saying "Now you have a place to live and a place to paint. I hope you will do lots of good work." Once a week he would come by and take the young artist to dinner, where she was introduced to Kiesler's friends, including Billy Rose, Franz Kline and Philip Guston. Toward the end of the non-resident term, Kiesler invited Johanson to work on *The Shrine of the Book*, the museum he was designing in Israel to house the Dead Sea Scrolls. Kiesler thought Johanson could do a wonderful job designing the garden for the project,[2] but the young artist felt frightened and overwhelmed by the idea. She returned to school.

After graduating from Bennington, Johanson enrolled in the graduate art history program at Hunter College in New York City. She was already defining her own pathway. She wanted no more studio training with "critiques, where some presumed master tells you what you are doing wrong." Johanson took only one studio course at Hunter, with Tony Smith, who had also been her teacher at Bennington. Johanson and Smith shared a passion for ideas and discussion. They were both interested in art and architecture, and in expanding and merging the boundaries of these disciplines. At that time, Smith had yet to conceive of the monumental sculptures for which he is best-known. "We had a close personal relationship," Johanson recalls. "I knew Tony in a host of ways, as a teacher, and as a person with major connections in the art world. He was always interesting to listen to. I also knew him socially, because he was dating girls my age, many of whom were fellow students." Johanson's friendship with Tony Smith continued right up until his death in 1980. During the Hunter College days Smith would often end up drinking in Johanson's studio late at night.

Smith taught a number of remarkable students at Hunter College, including Johanson, conceptual artist Robert Barry, painter Robert Huot, Minimal artist Robert Morris, and metal sculptor Tony Milkowski. Johanson says of her teacher: "Tony felt real pressure. We were all independent and self-directed. We were listening to what he said, but not necessarily accepting his pronouncements. This was a tough group of kids to teach. We were all on the verge of professional success, even though we were very young." Johanson remembers that Robert Morris had his first exhibition at the Green Gallery while he was a student in Tony's class. "Up to that point Tony was best-known for his domestic architecture. After he saw Bob Morris' exhibition, Tony became galvanized."

In 1964 Johanson was included in the first exhibition of "Minimal Art," Eugene Goossen's "8 Young Artists" at the Hudson River Museum. Later, she had group and solo shows at the Tibor de Nagy Gallery in New York. In 1968 Johanson's painting *William Clark* was included in "The Art of the Real," an exhibition organized by the Museum of Modern Art and traveling to prestigious venues around the world.[3] The painting was 28 feet long, with four aqua spots of color set within an orange line. The blue spots diminished in space when the painting was viewed from either end. When seen from the center, the painting engaged the viewer's peripheral sight and moved beyond the field of vision. *San Francisco Chronicle* reviewer Alfred Frankenstein saw the painting and wrote, "I have no idea if Miss Johanson is referring to William Clark of the Lewis and Clark expedition, but I have never had such an exhilarating journey through the imagination as in this painting."[4] Johanson remembers her delight that the implications of the painting's title had been recognized. "My work was always moving beyond the horizon," she says. "There's always something around the bend – where is it going? What is it doing?"[5]

Despite her success, Johanson found herself becoming increasingly impatient with the tiny world of art and its "self-congratulatory prattle." Her ideas were reaching out into the whole world, and she became engaged in design, architecture and urban planning. Frustrated by tradespeople who would not take her seriously, Johanson returned again to school in 1971. She entered the City College of New York and earned an architectural degree that gave her the technical background she needed to build big projects.

While studying at City College, Johanson found employment with the prestigious architectural firm Mitchell-Giurgola. In 1971, Romaldo Giurgola met Johanson and became familiar with her large-scale sculpture. He felt Johanson's work had important implications for architecture. While at Mitchell-Giurgola, Johanson worked as a site planner for an 80-acre park surrounding the Con Edison nuclear generating facility in Buchanan, New York. Using a mastodon footprint and a snake as the basis for her designs, Johanson conceived of interlocking concrete units which could be joined to form a bridge, overlook and continuous pathway, and then be stacked into stairways and plazas, assuming various sculptural configurations. The architects at Mitchell-Giurgola were excited by her designs.

Johanson laughs: "Giurgola was the dean at Columbia University Architecture School, which was a much more prestigious place than City College. He kept saying 'Come to Columbia! You can teach my students so much! I will make you an architect!' But I knew I was never going to be an architect. I just wanted to learn how to build large-scale constructions." Johanson collaborated on three projects with Mitchell-Giurgola, including the Con Edison site plan, a pavement design for Yale University and a sculptural landscape commissioned by Cummins Engine for Columbus East High School in Indiana. But her flourishing career as a designer for a major architectural firm was interrupted when Johanson became pregnant. "I've always abandoned success," she muses.

Goossen was horrified by her pregnancy. Johanson remembers: "I was not going to have an abortion. I was absolutely clear about that. It was at that point he really turned on me." Johanson kept working and attending school. She recalls actually being in labor while delivering a final report on concrete technology.

Eventually Goossen decided that Johanson should move to Buskirk, while he continued to work in New York City and visited her on weekends. Johanson remembers: "It was to be my punishment. I was cut off from everybody, my former life, the New York parties and friends, the art world, the galleries and museums. Buskirk is a very lonely

Bruised face, c. 1975
(photo: Michael Marton)

place. The house was on a dirt road; there were no neighbors. In those days there were cows out in the field. I was banished to Buskirk. But the funny thing is it worked very well for me. I loved it!" She laughs: "I've always been able to use anything to my advantage. I don't just roll over and die. So there I was in Buskirk with this baby – I didn't even drive at the time. I was totally isolated, half the time with not enough to eat in the house, but I was very happy. The baby and I were a unit, and it was the whole world."

Goossen was drinking heavily and often enraged at Johanson. "Part of the problem is if people are unhappy, they blame you," she says. "And I think that it can enrage a person who thinks you should be dependent, when clearly you're not." Eventually Goossen divorced his wife. He and Johanson married and had two more children. Goossen was physically violent towards Johanson from her first pregnancy in 1973 through the early years of their third son, some seven years later. One Monday after his weekend visit she went to the state police. Her face was battered and bruised. She asked the police what she could do. The following weekend, two officers came to the house and picked up her husband. She does not know what they said to him, but after that, the beatings ceased. These incidents tempered Johanson's love, but she chose to stay with her husband, knowing she could not hope to provide adequately for her three children on her own. Gradually, she gained more power and control in the relationship.

From 1966 to 1975, Johanson was engaged in building large-scale outdoor projects, beginning with the 200-foot-long sculpture *William Rush* (1966), and then with the 1600-foot sculpture *Stephen Long* (1968). She followed these monumental works with *Ixion's Wheel* (1969), a duodecagon sculpture, 1300 feet in circumference, installed at the State University of New York in Albany. *Cyrus Field*, built from 1970 to 1971, involved 70 tons of marble and miles of redwood and cement block. Johanson was used to working from dawn until dusk, handling dangerous equipment and heavy materials, and directing large crews of men. Then, in 1973, her first son Alvar was born. She says wryly, "I knew my work had to stop or change."

Johanson kept working in the only way she could. During brief snatches of time

Johanson with baby Nathaniel, 1981

while her baby napped, she sketched plants she would encounter during the long, exhausting day. With these tiny drawings, just one or two inches high, she would focus her attention on the plants, asking questions about them, and coming to understand why they looked the way they did. In the evenings she would take these tiny drawings and try to visualize the plants as built structures. As she stayed up through the night translating the little sketches into large architectural plans, she found the strategies of nature could be used to design unique and beautiful bridges, plazas, stairways and parks.

"One key benefit I have in all my parks is that I've spent so much time observing my own children, which is invaluable when you design public spaces," Johanson comments. "I wasn't charging ahead in New York and having exhibits in galleries, but discovering how children act at different ages prepared me for the next stage in my career." Johanson bought botany texts to study the plants that so engaged her, learning about their structures and functions.

"In a way, the whole process has been one of unlearning everything I was taught about art in school," she reflects. "When Alvar was born, I had to remove myself from the creative moment, the dependence on inspiration – in order to keep working. I began to render nature in a very straightforward way in the plant drawings. And I found everything in nature far more exciting than anything I could invent."

Johanson with her three sons, Alvar, Gerrit and Nathaniel Goossen in Buskirk, 1987

As she enjoyed her own children and immersed herself in the natural world, Johanson felt reconnected with her own childhood experience. Although she grew up in Brooklyn and New York City, Johanson remembers daily visits to the park, where she often made friends with park animals. She says, "If you think about what you see in an urban situation, those are really the strongest connections to nature for most people – not some grand national park, but the gardens that occur in the cracks of sidewalks, the squirrels that get to know you, the little mounds of sand with ants running in and out of the central hole. Like many children I spent hours looking at these small things." Her family had picnics in the park every weekend. "We lived in a small apartment with no space, and we had nowhere else to go," Johanson says. She also remembers visits to museums, and particularly a display of tiny Inuit carvings at the Brooklyn Museum: "I remember being glued to the glass showcases. I had never imagined anything like this. Carvings of animals – walruses and bears – moving over the topography of bones and tusks. It was magical to me." These early experiences shaped Johanson's commitment to public art and democratic access. She says, "Part of my insistence on making these projects public is that I know there are other children out there like me who will catch a vision, and that it will really affect their lives."

One weekend in 1976, Johanson attended a party at Herbert Ferber's house in South Egremont, Massachusetts with Goossen and their young son Alvar. Alvar, crawling at the time, attached himself to a woman's leg. As Johanson struggled to detach her child, the woman looked down at her imperiously and asked, "Who are you?" When Johanson introduced herself, the woman exclaimed, "I have been looking all over New

York for you! I am an art dealer, Rosa Esman, and I want to exhibit your work. Do you have any work?" Johanson described the drawings of plants she had been making.

Years after dropping out of the art scene in New York City, Johanson had acquired a prestigious 57th Street gallery. Esman framed the *Plant Drawings*, published a catalogue and mounted an exhibition. The show led to Johanson's first major commission for a large-scale public project at Fair Park Lagoon, when Harry Parker, Director of the Dallas Museum of Art, visited the gallery. Johanson laughs: "It would be very difficult to trudge around with your slides, and try to show them to dealers. But my child attacks a woman, and I am offered a 57th street exhibit and a multi-million dollar project!" Although Parker initially had no funds to commission a project, he was able to raise millions of dollars by exhibiting Johanson's conceptual project drawings at the museum. "It all goes back to Alvar attaching himself to this woman's leg! Some people plan their moves carefully. I've always done what I wanted, and then been very lucky," she says.

Johanson reflects on the happenstance behind much success, saying, "It's always interesting to me how careers are born and how success occurs. It never hurts to plan, and it's important to assemble your credentials. But the reality of why things turn out the way they do and what generates people's actions is often so casual."

Johanson remembers how Tony Smith first conceived of the large-scale minimalist sculpture for which he is so well-known. "One night he was sitting in my studio. He sat there with his drink, staring at a little black card-file box that was on the desk. Later that night, at 3 or 4 o'clock in the morning, the phone rang, and it was Smith. He had just returned to South Orange, New Jersey, and he wanted to know the exact dimensions of the card file box." Johanson staggered out of bed and measured it. This became the basis for Smith's first piece of monumental Minimalist sculpture, titled *The Black Box*. Johanson muses, "I'm not sure he ever would have taken that step, if he hadn't been surrounded by such a competitive, determined group of students."

While completing her masters degree in American art history, Johanson worked at the Frick Art Reference Library researching and writing a compendium of eighteenth and nineteenth century American artists for the publisher Benjamin Blom. A librarian

Johanson with Georgia O'Keeffe and son Alvar, Abiquiu, New Mexico, 1976

at the Frick recommended Johanson to artist Georgia O'Keeffe, who was looking for someone to catalogue her work. Johanson accompanied O'Keeffe to New Mexico, and she and the elder artist began a lifelong friendship that still inspires Johanson. "I loved O'Keeffe's painting and her simple lifestyle, but she was also the mentor who could tell me how it was done," Johanson says.

Comparing her relationship with Georgia O'Keeffe to her friendship with Helen Frankenthaler, Johanson notes: "Frankenthaler and I had a strong personal relationship, but while I admire her paintings enormously, I knew I could never follow in her footsteps." Frankenthaler was a wealthy woman from a powerful New York family. She was associated with two influential men, Clement Greenberg and Robert Motherwell. She was a very social person who held lavish parties where art-world luminaries would meet and mix. Johanson identified much more closely with Georgia O'Keeffe. "O'Keeffe and I were both outsiders," Johanson says. "We both had the determination to achieve success on our own terms. Neither of us was going to follow the established route or jump through any of the hoops that were set up for us. What I loved about O'Keeffe is that whenever she decided something wasn't working for her, she had no compunction about going off and following a different path. She was fiercely independent."

While Johanson enjoyed an intimate friendship with Helen Frankenthaler, "I never aspired to *be* Frankenthaler. On the other hand, I knew I *was* O'Keeffe." Johanson laughs, remembering long evenings at Abiquiu where she and O'Keeffe would munch minutely on their dinners, both of them very slow eaters. "O'Keeffe wanted to tell me about men, life, art, careers and money. She wanted to tell me how to be a success, but that you should never give up what you cared about. I felt like the daughter she never had. The daughter she would have wanted would be exactly like herself – somebody who was bent on success, and bent on doing it her own way. That was our bond."

Johanson admired the way O'Keeffe kept challenging herself, studying and exploring new interests throughout her entire life. At O'Keeffe's home in the New Mexico desert, Johanson found stacks of current *Art News*, *Artforum* and *Art In America* carefully annotated by the solitary artist. O'Keeffe read these magazines carefully, and stayed passionately interested in what was going on in New York. One night over dinner she asked Johanson: "Do you think I could paint a big painting? I think I should paint a big painting but I don't know how to do it." She showed Johanson a small maquette of *Above the Clouds*, and Johanson put her in touch with a specialist who fabricated a 24-foot stretcher for her.

"O'Keeffe always had the ability to make these radical switches, following what she needed at any given moment, what nourished her," Johanson says. "I think that's very sound advice for all of us. She loved older men when she was younger. Of course, as a young person you want to be with somebody who can feed your interests, tell you what you need to know, and help advance your career. Then by the time I knew her, she was involved with very young men. Part of that, I think, was that she now knew exactly what she wanted. She didn't need anybody giving her advice and telling her what to do. So while it may have seemed like a radical switch to a lot of people – it made perfect sense to me." Johanson laughs: "Perhaps men had become decorative objects. Her real love was her art."

Johanson was inspired by O'Keeffe's humble life, far removed from art-world glamour. O'Keeffe walked each day in the desert, tended an organic garden, enjoyed good food and wine, and took care of the people and animals around her. Johanson has followed a similar pathway. She identifies with O'Keeffe's love of nature, and her separation from both New York City and her husband. "When she discovered Stieglitz was cheating on her, she moved out. She didn't get a divorce – that wouldn't have been to her advantage. She drove out to New Mexico one day, fell in love with it, and had her belongings shipped west. Only a very strong person can do that."

When Johanson first met O'Keeffe, the elder artist's career was in eclipse. She was little known outside of a loyal older following in Los Angeles and New York. Johanson introduced O'Keeffe to Goossen, who wrote a profile of the artist for *Vogue* magazine. The magazine sent photographer Cecil Beaton to O'Keeffe's New Mexico homes in Abiquiu and Ghost Ranch, where he took a series of photographs that immortalized the strong-featured artist posed next to a cow skull, and striding through the desert with her walking stick. Suddenly O'Keeffe became a national icon and a heroine to young women in the nascent feminist movement.

One piece of O'Keeffe's advice that Johanson did not follow involved dress and personal style. Stieglitz encouraged O'Keeffe to become recognizable through the way she dressed in public. The artist had an austere black outfit she always wore for photographs and public appearances. O'Keeffe advised Johanson to become "as much of an image as the work itself." But Johanson's style is quiet and anonymous.

"I'm a bit of a voyeur. I like to be an anonymous person so that I can observe everything that's going on around me," Johanson says. She designs her work so that the art disappears and visitors become engaged with nature. She dislikes having her name included on her sculptures. She explains, "I'm just a workman! I'm just somebody who envisions these projects. I don't need anyone to treat me as though I'm special." Her style reflects her democratic values, and perhaps is shaped by her commitment to the world of insects, worms, algae and microorganisms.

In 1989, when Johanson was 48 years old, she traveled to New York for a routine medical checkup. With thirty-two enlarged lymph nodes, advanced cancer was immediately diagnosed. The doctor told Johanson she would likely die within six months. Johanson first had to find an oncologist who would agree to treat her, and then endure a year and a half of chemotherapy and radiation treatments. Simultaneously, she researched alternative therapies, and read about the herbal anti-cancer formula "essiac." Johanson ordered dried herbs from Canada and boiled them into a tea. She took this formula for many years, while subsisting on a diet that consisted of little more than raw, organic vegetables. Johanson beat all the odds and survived.

Today, Johanson is free of cancer, and she sees the ordeal as a positive experience. She was moved by her parents' support. Of her children, she muses, "When they were told that their

Cancer, 1989
(photo: Alvar Goossen)

mother could die and had to witness the effects of the cancer treatments, they were devastated. I think it changed their lives even more than it changed mine." Johanson says that cancer has given her a deeper understanding of life. Her survival left her feeling both blessed and empowered – ready to travel the world and address global issues with her art.

Johanson says artists who want to make a difference should keep their goals high and their personal needs at a minimum. "Never believe that money is the solution," she insists. "It is your ability as a creative person to envision positive change that will make a difference." While she feels deeply grateful for the support she has received from the Guggenheim and Gottlieb Foundations, the National Endowment for the Arts and the Arts and Healing Network, she also worked for many years without realizing any income from her work.

"I don't think an artist's work should ever be linked to financial sustenance," she says. "You need to proceed with or without financial support." For Johanson, it has been important to keep working in any way possible, never succumbing to discouragement. Her commitment to art-making has never wavered since her freshman year at Bennington, no matter what twists and turns her life has taken.

"Even if nobody is interested in your ideas, you can still write and draw. I consider the small drawings I made in the 1960s my most important work." For Johanson, moving from drawings and ideas to creating built structures in the real world took decades

Johanson in Kenya, 1996
(photo: Nathaniel Goossen)

of patient persistence. For many years, she had to sustain her energy and self-confidence in solitude, simply through the excitement of doing significant work. "When the plant drawings were exhibited there were a couple of people who realized they were buildable projects – and that's all you need. You don't need a whole lot of support. If you find one person who understands what you are doing, that's all that matters."

Throughout her career, Johanson has faced many obstacles, but she has managed to find in each an opportunity. An impoverished childhood was far from deprived – as time spent in public parks and museums was vital to shaping her ideas and values. Her family's sacrifices and support while she attended college meant "there was no possibility that I would ever flunk out. I couldn't have let my family down." When she had to finance her own postgraduate studies, she began her work for an art publisher, and because she spent so many hours a day in research libraries, she was recommended to O'Keeffe. Johanson exclaims: "Imagine a young woman in her twenties able to go off to New Mexico with Georgia O'Keeffe!"

Johanson remembers that when she first saw Frankenthaler after becoming pregnant, "Frankenthaler said, 'Well, that's the end of that.' She meant that my brilliant art career was at an end. But in a sense it was just beginning." Being separated from the art world and consumed by the urgencies of motherhood provided information Johanson draws on in all her work. Living in the country allowed her to reconnect with nature and "my sense of wonder at the simplicity, complexity, elegance and significance of nature has never ceased. It is clearly an inexhaustible textbook and source."[6] The enforced isolation allowed Johanson to refine her unique creative voice.

"I think whatever happens to you, if you're a creative person you use it to best advantage. There's nothing that's totally negative." Johanson's difficult marriage provided financial security for her children and herself, while she stayed detached from the emotional entanglements that keep others from risk and achievement. Her battle with cancer has informed all her subsequent work, sharpening her focus on survival. Her husband's death and ensuing financial obligations led to her accepting larger, more lucrative projects around the world.

Although Johanson has faced many obstacles as a woman artist, she feels her gender also offers many advantages. As feminism emerged, Johanson received support from many women with an interest in female artists and galleries that wanted to show more work by women. Her inclusion in Eleanor Munro's book, *Originals: American Women Artists*, in 1979 helped Johanson become known around the world. Feminist art magazines *Heresies* and *Gallerie* featured her art and writing. Johanson sees her practice as one which is deeply informed by gender. "I think women are good at juggling complex, conflicting situations. We're good at seeing many different points of view simultaneously. It seems we have less need to deal with the world in terms of imposed structures. We have an ability to negotiate our way through the world creatively, because we've always had to. Women are committed to life, and to perpetuating life."

Johanson believes that artists who work in the public realm must accept compromise and forgo perfection. She applies these same lessons to her own life, saying: "There are people like me who think they can do everything, and try to do it, and then make the necessary compromises as they go along. You can never have it all, but you can certainly have parts of it all. And that's more-or-less what I've done. I must say it fits in with my approach to the work. This great stew is always brewing, and there are all these parts that interweave and combine. Ultimately, you come up with something that's complex and unexpected, rather than simple and straightforward."

When Johanson was young she received the support of many established artists. Today, she is pleased to offer help to others. She speculates that her mentors must have found her "relentless." She saw all their shows, read about their work and cared deeply about what they had to say. "I think what they saw in me was dedication. I think it struck a chord in them. Nobody ever gets anywhere in life without having that kind of devotion to cause and determination to see it through." Today she can recognize

Top left: Feeding squirrels in Highland Park, 1942

Right: Family bungalow in Catskill Mountains, New York, with great-grandmother Olivia Carlsen

Below: Johanson with her mother, Elizabeth Deane Johanson, in Highland Park, c. 1943

those same qualities in a few of the many students who contact her with requests. "There are always two or three every year that touch my heart. I take them under my wing, do what I can – but not with all of them. The ones who are just writing a paper, and who don't really care, I help in a more routine

Johanson speaking at Wuhan University, China, 2004 (photo: Rick Benitez)

way. But some of the others – I've really followed a couple of careers. I see how dedicated they are and how hard they work. I know that they're going to do something in this field."

From her student days, Johanson has created work that is clearly art but very different from the art around her. "My dialogue wasn't with other art," she says. "It was always with something else out in the world. That is really what unites all my work – I'm always engaged in a conversation with something else that's out there." Today, she looks for these same qualities in the people she reaches out to help. "People who are focused on trying to be like me are not the ones who would be of interest to me. Some artists just want to imitate what I've done – but that isn't necessary! What I always look for are people who are dedicated, committed and hard workers – people who want to follow their own path. You know that they'll go on and do something with their lives. You don't know what, but it doesn't matter. Those are the people who are really worth helping."

Johanson likens her journey as an artist to finding her way along a mountain trail. "One of the things you discover as you grow older is that everything is important. You learn to appreciate everything for what it is – the successes as well as the failures. It's not as though you can just keep climbing straight to the top of the mountain. People who want to zoom to the top are doomed to failure. There are many conflicting and overlapping concerns and realities. You need to move carefully to find your way."

Caffyn Kelley and Patricia Johanson

Now in her mid-sixties, Johanson approaches the future with the same openness, honesty and willingness that have characterized her life to date. She says, "I will be happy going in any direction. People think that careers should only move in one direction, that they have to always 'progress' to something bigger – more land, more money, more success. I have never felt that way." She considers that she might well make tiny drawings again, and work only in the realm of ideas, questioning whether she will have time and energy for more big projects.

Johanson is now caring for aging parents and she nurtures her grown sons. She describes family as "the core of who you are. You cannot leave your family behind to become something better. And – just as in my landscapes – you cannot only take the 'good' parts and leave out the parts you don't like."

Johanson notes that as people are connected with their families, so are landscapes connected with their origins and history. She describes an intimate relationship between specific places and the human interventions that are possible in any location. Hence the importance of listening to each landscape and learning its stories. Without this attention to the specifics of a location, human effort can literally be mis-placed. She cites the example of prairie farmers, plowing up native perennial grasses in order to plant wheat. They applied themselves to their project with such hard work and enormous sacrifice, only to have the land turn to dust when it was no longer anchored by perennial grass roots. "I won't mind doing less as I get older," she says. "A path of more contemplation and less action is often the best one to take."

Today, Johanson receives many invitations to design large-scale public projects. She is continually asked to write, lecture and appear in exhibitions around the world. A bibliography[7] of writing on her work includes hundreds of articles, as well as television and radio interviews. She is frequently contacted by students researching her life and curators wanting to mount exhibits. Her work has been widely recognized by professional landscape architects. She served as the keynote speaker at the International Federation of Landscape Architects in Brazil in 2002. Her drawings have been collected by major museums, including the Metropolitan Museum of Art, New York, the Museum of Modern Art, New York, the National Museum of Women in the Arts in Washington, D.C., and the Dallas Museum of Art. Johanson describes these professional achievements as "a parallel track that doesn't affect me at all." She stresses: "What is important is doing the work. For every artist that's the key – you have to figure out how to create the work, how to support it yourself, and how to keep going out and presenting it." Remembering how Georgia O'Keeffe continued working in solitude and obscurity, Johanson reflects that recognition by galleries and museums may never come, or it may not last a lifetime.

Johanson's unwavering commitment is to art and survival. She proves that artists can become more than "purveyors of objects to an audience that is too small and too wealthy." She designs places of beauty and life-sustaining habitat, where birds nest and children play. Her work suggests multiple ways we might reinvent the relationship between culture and nature, while proposing a new vision for public space. In tiny drawings and in parks covering hundreds of acres, Johanson shows how art can actually transform the world.

NOTES:

1 E.C. Goossen, 1959, "The End of the Object," *Art International*, vol. 3 no. 8, p. 42.

2 The Billy Rose Sculpture Garden, later designed by Isamu Noguchi.

3 Including the Grand Palais, Paris, Kunsthaus, Zurich, and the Tate Gallery in London, England.

4 Alfred Frankenstein, July 21, 1968, "New York Collects," *San Francisco Examiner and Chronicle*, pp. 37-38.

5 In 2004 a similar painting, *Minor Keith*, was included in "A Minimal Future? Art as Object: 1958-1968," curated by Ann Goldstein at the Museum of Contemporary Art in Los Angeles. Reviewer Michael Kimmelman wrote, "Presence is everything with this art. You have to walk past that long blue line that Ms. Johanson painted on a bare canvas at eye level – a bodily allusion – to measure its length in time and experience it as quasi-architecture.... The tug of an art that unapologetically sees itself as on a par with science and religion is not to be underestimated either." "How not much is a whole world," April 2, 2004, *New York Times*, pp. B-29, B-31.

6 Johanson, interviewed by D. Hobson, 2003, "An Interview with Patricia Johanson, Recipient of the 2003 Arts and Healing Network Award," retrieved September 2003 from the Arts and Healing Network News Archive at www.artheals.org.

7 See Johanson's website: www.patriciajohanson.com for a select bibliography and other information on Johanson's projects.

SELECT BIBLIOGRAPHY OF WRITINGS BY PATRICIA JOHANSON

Johanson, P. 1969. "House and Garden manuscripts" unpublished manuscripts

Johanson, P. 1973 . "Patricia Johanson, A Selected Retrospective: 1959-1973," (catalogue). Bennington, Vermont: Bennington College

Johanson, P. 1974. " Patricia Johanson: Some Approaches to Landscape, Architecture and the City," (catalogue). New Jersey: Montclair State College

Johanson, P. 1978. "Patricia Johanson: Plant Drawings for Projects," (catalogue). New York: Rosa Esman Gallery

Johanson, P. 1985 . "Architecture as Landscape," *The Princeton Journal*, New Jersey: Princeton Architectural Press

Johanson, P. 1986. "Toward a New Art," paper presented at the inauguration of Fair Park Lagoon, Dallas. Patricia Johanson Papers, Archives of American Art, Smithsonian Institution, Washington, D.C.

Johanson, 1991. "Patricia Johanson: Public Landscapes," (catalogue). Philadelphia: Painted Bride Art Center

Johanson, P. 1992. *Art and Survival: Creative Solutions to Environmental Problems*. North Vancouver: Gallerie Publications. Women Artists' Monographs Series, Issue 8

Johanson, P. 1996 (a). "Art and Ecology: The Battle for Nairobi River," *Bennington Magazine*, Vol. 28, No. 2

Johanson, P. 1996 (b) "Nature/Culture/Aesthetics/Function," in Ulsan Park: What is a Park for the 21st Century? Proceedings of International Symposium, Yukong, Seoul, South Korea, August 19-24

Johanson, P. 1997. "Preserving Biocultural Diversity in Public Parks," *NAPtexts: A Literary Journal* (New Arts Program, Kutztown, Pennsylvania), Vol. 2, No. 2

Johanson, P. 1998. "Brockton Reborn: The City as an Ecological Art Form." *Sanctuary: The Journal of the Massachusetts Audubon Society*, Vol. 38, No. 2

Facing page: *Fair Park Lagoon*
(Photo: Elizabeth Duvert)

Johanson, P. 1999. "La Ville Comme Forme D'Art Ecologique: La Trace de Rocky Marciano," *Les Annales de la Recherche Urbaine*, No. 85, Paris, France

Johanson, P. February 24, 2000. "Designing Beyond the Visual: Life, Death, and Trade-Offs in the Garden of Art." Speech to College Art Association, Audio Archives, La Crescenta, California, Audiotape 200223-190 A & B

Johanson, P. 2000. "Beyond Choreography: Shifting Experiences in Uncivilized Gardens," manuscript for talk given at the Symposium on Landscape Design and the Experience of Motion, Studies in Landscape Architecture, Dumbarton Oaks, Washington, D.C., May 19-20, 2000

Johanson, P. 2003. "Beyond Choreography: Shifting Experiences in Uncivilized Gardens," in: Michel Conan, ed., *Landscape Design and the Experience of Motion*, Washington, D.C.: Dumbarton Oaks

Johanson, P. Summer 2003. "Fecund Landscapes: Art and Process in Public Parks," *Landscape and Art*, (London: UK) Number 29. Reprinted in: *Beauty and the Way of Modern Life*, China: Wuhan University Press, 2004

INDEX TO MAJOR PROJECTS